TOXIC

Also by Neil Ruddock

Hell Razor: The Autobiography

The World According to Razor: My Closest Shaves

TOXIC

Tackling 'Razor' and Finding the Real Me

NEIL RUDDOCK

HEADLINE

First published in 2024 by
HEADLINE PUBLISHING GROUP

1

Cataloguing in Publication Data is available from the British Library.

Hardback ISBN 978 1 0354 1954 8

Printed and bound in Great Britain by Clays Ltd, Elcograf S.p.A.

Headline's policy is to use papers that are natural, renewable and recyclable
products and made from wood grown in well-managed forests and other
controlled sources. The logging and manufacturing processes are expected
to conform to the environmental regulations of the country of origin.

HEADLINE PUBLISHING GROUP
An Hachette UK Company
Carmelite House
50 Victoria Embankment
London EC4Y 0DZ

www.headline.co.uk
www.hachette.co.uk

For Leah, Pebbles, Kizzy, Joshua and Millie.

This is for you.

I love you all so much.

CONTENTS

PROLOGUE

Razor Ruddock – who is he? It's a question I've been asking myself a lot. You'd think I'd know by now. After all, I've been around the bloke a long time. When I started out as Razor, the mullet was in fashion, women danced round their handbags and Chris de Burgh was banging on about that 'Lady In Red'. For years he's been my best mate – Razor, not Chris de Burgh. There's scrapes me and him have got into that would make your hair, and other things, curl. I'll tell you some of them shortly – apologies to past teammates who've woken up without eyebrows/life savings/a house.

Thing is, recently I've come to realise that Razor isn't really me anymore. Or rather he'd turned me into a cartoon version of myself. A cartoon where all the laughter seemed to have stopped.

There was one particular snapshot of Razor that halted me in my tracks – a picture I found on my phone. There, sat beneath a pub dartboard, was a sunken-eyed, grey-haired man with his belly round his knees. It took me a few looks before I recognised who it was. Sounds daft, I know, but honest to God it was that big a shock. The only slightly amusing thing was my classic 'What the fuck!' double take.

It really was like looking at a stranger. So much had changed. Where once there was fun and mischief in those eyes, now there was total emptiness. Same with the trademark Razor grin. Gone. Replaced by a blank weariness.

You'd think I had the weight of the world on my shoulders. And looking back at that photo now, I can see I did. This was the face of someone who'd reached the end of the road. Lost, tired, devoid of all energy. Past caring. If I'd been a dog – a proper dog, big and hairy, not something stupid like a chihuahua – people would have been saying I should be put out of my misery. And I'd have agreed. Certainly, my days of haring across fields chasing a ball were long gone. In fact, if I'm totally honest, a trip to the vet right there and then didn't seem a bad idea. Saying goodbye to the emptiness? The misery? Bring it on. The ninety minutes was up and I didn't feel much like playing extra time. There'd been too many head-in-hands moments. Too much trying to be someone I wasn't.

PROLOGUE

It had gone on for years and years. Initially, booze had fuelled that alter ego, and then, as I started to dislike myself more and more, I'd piled into the food. I was once the fittest bloke you'd met. I didn't play for some of the biggest clubs out there for nothing. A lot of people remember me for being a hardman, but you can't be a hardman without being fit – if you're going to snap someone's ankles you've got to catch them first. Now all I was running towards was a cliff face. The personality I'd created all those years ago had finally caught up. And it wanted to shove me into the abyss.

Initially, I'd thought this big, brash, noisy bloke – funny, never switched off, always in the thick of the action – would help me fit in when it came to the harsh world of football. People might ask why I needed to go to such extremes, but to me, Razor was born out of necessity. As a kid everyone was older than me. I had big brothers, and then, as soon as I showed an ability at football, I was playing against more senior lads and men. If I wanted to be noticed, as a player and a person, I needed a voice. Well, a foghorn really. That basically was the birth of Razor. The bloke who, if there were twenty other players in the pub, everyone wanted to be with – and then regretted it the next day. If Razor was a drink, I reckon most people would see him as a pint of lager – straight up and down, no messing. But to me, Razor was actually more like a whisky chaser – good fun until you're sick on the carpet.

For a while, Razor worked like a dream. Or at least I thought he did. He got me noticed, on and off the pitch. Everyone wanted to be my mate. Everyone wanted to have a drink with me. Everyone told me I was great. But when everything's laid on a plate, the ingredients are often toxic. At the heart of that toxicity was the fact that Razor was the go-to character for me and everyone else around me. Everyone wanted Razor to be the life and soul – the loudest, the one who could drink the most, the one who made something happen. If something mad went down on a night out, there could only ever be one reason – Razor turned up. I'm the prime example of a man who bottled his reality away. Thankfully, I've learned to release the pressure. I don't have to put on an act.

Equally, it would be hypocritical of me to pretend that being Razor couldn't be fun, which was what made him so addictive. It wasn't like I was hooked on something that gave me only misery. If you're addicted to gambling, eventually you're going to end up with nothing. I don't look on Razor like that. There are good memories of the bloke. It's just that he was a ticking time bomb. There's a fuse running on a personality like that. Good luck trying to get out of the way when it blows up.

That explosion came in retirement. Instead of doing what I should have done and waved goodbye to Razor when I hung up my boots, I wore his mask more and more. Being me, and facing up to a post-career, everyday life as me, felt difficult enough as it was. If ever I needed a defence mechanism, now was it. No way could I just chuck Razor on the scrapheap. Let's be honest, it was much easier to be him than it was to be me. Razor was the one people liked, the one people asked for. The proof was in the pudding. When *I'm A Celebrity . . . Get Me Out Of Here!* came knocking, they didn't want Neil, they wanted Razor. Loud, full-on, happy to act the fool, make a joke out of anything, and down an ostrich anus smoothie – *that* Razor.

Again, I'm not saying that didn't have its plus-sides – maybe not the smoothie – but I was always aware there was another element to myself that others weren't seeing. In fact, only a trusted few had ever witnessed my more emotional side. I'm not alone in that approach, especially in football. I've known a lot of noisy footballers down the years, people who would never open up and admit there was more to them than meets the eye; that actually, mentally, they're in a world of trouble. So stuck in that zipped-up macho world are they that even when only their fingertips are showing they still won't admit the quicksand has got them.

Not that I fooled everyone. There's always been an astute few who could see that Razor was only part of me. Robbie Williams is a case in point. A few of the Liverpool lads used to see Rob a bit back in his Take That days and me and him always hit it off. Looking back now, I wonder if part of that was because we were both in industries where you've always got to wear a public face. I was Neil and Razor. He was Rob and Robbie. A few times, talking about his ups and downs with mental health, he actually warned me: 'Look, mate, don't be getting like me.' Even so, it took me a long time to understand what he really meant. I've always shied away from the word 'depression' – I suppose I've got an ingrained mindset of 'just get on with it'. But there have definitely been times when I've been what I prefer to call 'down in the dumps'. I'd have runs of days where I wouldn't go out, wouldn't do anything really. I'd be up for two hours and then just go back to bed.

Sometimes, especially when I thought about my children from my first marriage, who, after a particularly ugly divorce, I hadn't seen for years, I would find myself just staring at the floor. To have no idea what your children are doing, how they're growing up, how they look, who they're with, what they want to be, is like having a sharp knife pushed millimetre by millimetre into your guts. I'd find myself trying to summon up their faces, remember their voices. The biggest fear of all was that one day I'd wake up and those treasured bits of memory would have been stolen by time. Try as I might to find them, they just wouldn't be there.

To get through those daily tortures I needed my mind to be busy, to be doing something, anything, other than wallowing. Finding the willpower was the issue. Sat at home on my own was never a good place. That's when I'd disappear down the rabbit hole. Down there was the drink, the food, that delivered the temporary high. The next stage, of course, was the crushing low. I understand addiction. When you're in a pit of despair, you'll do anything to claw your way out again. But ultimately all you're doing is digging yourself deeper and deeper until one day the sides cave in and you're buried alive. Over time you come to view the world in a way that's totally upside down. More than once, for instance, I found myself yearning for another lockdown. I enjoyed those months. They were a blessed relief. A chance to sit at home, get lazier and lazier, and eat. I was using food in the same way I'd so often used booze – a comfort blanket to smother every mood, every emotion. I was destroying my physical health, because I had a problem with my mental health. The only difference was that with food I could destroy it alone.

With drink, first in the pub at 11 a.m., I'd wait until someone came in and drag them over to the bar. I was the best kidnapper in the world for quite a while. That's the thing with retiring from football; you go from having thirty mates in the dressing room, and thousands more singing your name on the terraces, to nothing at all. I wasn't the first, and I certainly won't be the last, to try to find that buzz at the bottom of a glass. Getting smashed and watching football on the telly was all I had. Always trying to recreate that high, the piss-taking, the camaraderie, that whole amazing thing of being part of a team. One minute you're the main course, the next you're on the compost pile. That's a big change for anybody to take on board. Not many people are equipped to deal with it. And, for the benefit of anyone who's never found themselves in that situation, let me tell you, it's lonely. Very lonely indeed. No time to be ditching a pal like Razor who could slide seamlessly into any social situation. 'Mad, bad, sad, glad syndrome,' I called it. No matter how I was feeling I reached for the same old answer – the mask of Razor and a big night out.

PROLOGUE

If that awful picture on my phone had not acted as a wake-up call, I don't know what would have happened. I'll be straight, there've been times when I've wondered if it wouldn't be a whole lot easier for everyone if I wasn't around. When everything gets so complicated, you look for the easy way out. In the end, though, it was my physical, not mental, health that nearly killed me. I was two months away from death. If I had not found that out, I wouldn't be here now (no smart comments, please).

That's why you might have looked at the cover of this book and done your own double take. It's taken me a little while to come to terms with the new-look me too. But the new physical me 100 per cent represents the new mental me. I feel like a different person, because I am a different person. I'm half the man I used to be, but twice the man I used to be – finally able to be open and honest, with myself as well as those around me. The poison that was dripping into my mind and body has gone.

I don't ever want to go back to that old life. I had some great times being Razor, but there were too many nightmares as well. I'm not a churchgoer, but there were plenty of occasions when I'd look skywards and ask, 'God, please get me out of this situation.' Now I'm different. That doesn't mean Razor is no more. Far from it. He'll forever be part of me. But no longer does he define who I am. These days, as myself, I'm happy to go anywhere. My confidence and self-esteem have never been higher. I've thrown away the outsized clothes on that photo and with them chucked out the shamefaced person I'd become. I've worn a few different outfits down the years – Millwall, Southampton, Tottenham, Liverpool, West Ham and Crystal Palace spring to mind – but, finally, I'm happy in my own skin.

They say you have to hit rock bottom before you can start looking up. That didn't quite happen to me. I never played for Arsenal. But, joking apart, I am determined that my story should help others, men in particular, to open up about their problems, their feelings, before they find themselves totally caged in by their inability to speak.

I've come to see that me being a footballer was actually only one part of my own closed-upness. Like most blokes, it had more to do with not wanting to be seen as weak, which, let's face it, really means being open with our emotions. Strange, isn't it, that so many men are so hung up about so many things that they'd rather suffer alone than risk being judged – judgement which, I can tell you now, never comes. What you actually receive for opening up is respect, help, a second chance and a pathway to a better life. One where you can laugh, cry and everything in between – in this case hopefully at some of the mad, bad, sad and glad things you'll read over the next 300 or so pages.

For me, the reset button has been well and truly pressed. The bloke under the dartboard has disappeared, replaced by a man who likes himself.

I hope I can help other people, maybe you or someone you know, to like the real them too.

Neil 'Razor' Ruddock

September 2024

1

I'M SORRY, I DON'T KNOW HOW TO TELL YOU THIS . . .

If there was a trigger in my life for losing control as Neil and becoming peak, unrestrained, messed-up Razor, it was being dropped for the 1996 FA Cup Final. It was the worst thing anyone could have done to me, not just in football, but in life. From that point on, Razor unhitched from reality and became a runaway train.

The journey to that Cup Final didn't begin when Liverpool beat Rochdale 7–0 in the third round in January 1996; it began when West Ham beat Fulham in May 1975. That was the first Final I remember, and from that moment on playing at Wembley in the FA Cup Final was what I wanted more than anything else in the world. It was why, day after day, I used to get out of bed at some horrible time as a kid and run my bollocks off, constantly working hard, trying to get better and better. This, the FA Cup Final, was my ultimate goal. Even now, when I think back to being a kid and the FA Cup Final, I can feel the excitement in my bones. What a day that was.

Younger people might think what I'm saying is mad. In an era where finishing in the top four in the Premier League is everything, the FA Cup has been shoved to one side, a back-up if one of the big clubs looks like they're going to miss out. But when I was growing up, it was by miles the biggest sporting day of the year. Back then, it was the only live club game you saw on telly. BBC and ITV both showed it, with the build-up starting on the kids' shows at eight in the morning and lasting all day. There'd be a special FA Cup *A Question of Sport*, and even cameras on the coaches travelling to the ground from the team hotels. You'd see the approach to the stadium through the eyes of the players as they crawled through the fans outside and then into the bowels of Wembley itself. Not long after, they'd emerge onto the pitch, dressed in immaculate suits made especially for the big day, for a wave at the fans and a pre-match wander across the famous turf. About ten to three, the managers would lead their sides out. An absolute cauldron of noise. You'd see the players looking for family in the crowd as they made their way to the middle. You understood 100 per cent what this day meant to them. Chests out, pride in their eyes. Honestly, it sends a shiver down my spine thinking about it. The formalities would happen, meeting the dignitaries and all that, and then the whole place would belt out the National Anthem. The captains would swap pendants and off we'd go – the biggest game in club football, watched by millions across the world. I'd actually sat and watched this unfold from the side of the Wembley pitch as a teenager when Coventry beat Spurs in one of the great finals in 1987. I was in the Spurs first-team squad at the time, having made my debut in the quarter-final win at Wimbledon, and was in total awe of the occasion. In my book, the only bigger game in all football was the World Cup Final, and I was pretty sure I wasn't going to make it to that. But the FA Cup? If I worked hard, really pushed myself and did well enough, then it might just – just – be possible. Put it this way, it wasn't impossible. I could make it there, and if I did, it would be the biggest game of my life.

In 1996, that's exactly what it would – or should – have been. Not only was I going to play in the FA Cup Final, but it would be against Liverpool's biggest rivals, Manchester United. Me against Eric Cantona. I loved playing against Cantona. I got in his head and he didn't like it. I couldn't wait.

Roy Evans said he was going to name the team on the Thursday before the match. When he didn't, the lads just thought it was going to be the same side as the previous week. On that basis, I had no reason to believe that my number 25 shirt wouldn't be there hanging in the Wembley changing-room. I'd played in the quarter-final, a 3–0 win against Leeds, and the semi-final, a 3–0 demolition of Aston Villa when I was up against a strike force of Dwight Yorke and Savo Milosevic, plus the last six games of the league season, and yet at five o'clock on the Friday afternoon as we were finishing some last-minute training, Roy Evans wandered across and uttered the words that no pro ever wants to hear: 'I'm sorry. I don't know how to tell you this, but you're not in the team tomorrow.' And with that my world caved in. I didn't know what to do or say. 'Fuck off, gaffer,' I muttered and got on the coach. The moment I'd dreamed of being part of since a little kid was gone. At what felt like the last minute, I'd been denied the biggest day of my life. I could hardly find my seat through the tears.

Funnily enough, it was my birthday that day – definitely not one to remember. Instead of my dad wishing me happy returns and good luck for tomorrow, I had to tell him I wasn't playing. He'd got fifty tickets for the Final, invited all sorts of people to see his son play in the biggest game of them all, and then it had all vanished in a phone call. He had the job of ringing every one of those people and telling them. He didn't go to the match and neither did anyone else in my family. From a position where I felt like I'd made everybody so proud, I now felt like I'd let everybody down. Remember, reaching an FA Cup Final isn't like getting to the final of the World Darts Championship. You know for weeks that it's happening. All that time the excitement's building. Everyone's making plans. A big party at the back of the house for friends and family. A big celebratory get-together at the pub. Weeks and weeks of it – and then the night before, for everyone, it's all gone. Dad never spoke about it. I didn't expect or want him to. I knew, like me, he was totally devastated. That Cup Final might not have been the greatest football game ever, but it would certainly have been the greatest football game he'd ever go to.

At the hotel later that night, the lads brought me a birthday cake. They could see how devasted I was and shoved it in my face, trying to make me laugh. I appreciated what they were trying to do and did my best to join in, but it was all a front. Missing out hurt – a lot. My first thought was not to eat cake but to get obliterated, although in the end I only had a couple of beers that night and went to bed. The day after was going to be the tough one. While I wished every one of them well, being in and around the lads as they got ready was going to be torture. I knew I'd be ticking off every landmark, held in my head since I was a kid. Board the coach to Wembley – tick. Drive up to the stadium through the fans – tick. Walk out on to the pitch – tick. There was only one way I was ever going to deal with all that and so even before kick-off I was on the drink. Reaching for something to take the pain away, I sat on my own in a corner of the changing room. You might not have known I was there but for the clicking open of lager cans. Not the done thing, I'm sure, but everyone knew to leave me alone.

When the players walked onto the pitch in Liverpool's green and white second strip to the sound of the band of The Blues and Royals and the Life Guards playing 'Abide With Me', another part of Cup Final tradition I'd always loved, I joined them at the back of the line before veering off and heading to the bench in an already notoriously naff cream suit which I'd happily have chucked in the nearest bin. For me, that suit will always be associated with the worst memory of my footballing life. I'd been dropped from the team but still had to walk out in it and look proud of being part of the big day. I had to take it on the chin and show respect. Which I did, even though I'd have been a lot happier had the ground just swallowed me up and spat me out 200 miles away in a bar on Merseyside.

At half-time with the game at 0–0, I followed the lads into the dressing room and, while the boss gave his instructions, cracked open another lager. I didn't care what that looked like. What was anyone going to do about it? I'd had my dream taken away from me. There's no greater punishment than that. Don't get me wrong, I still desperately wanted the lads to win, but I needed that bit of mental detachment to get me through the day.

The Final itself was one of the worst for years. The commentator Barry Davies summed it up – 'John Barnes led a side that was almost unrecognisable from the side that has thrilled so often this season.' United won 1–0 and with it the Double. Cantona, naturally, scored the goal. I'm not saying it would have been different with me in the team, but even if I'd played and lost it would have been better than not playing at all. Don't play and you're left in limbo. You'll never know what might have happened. All I could do was stand by the tunnel watching the team receive their losers' medals. I didn't want a loser's medal any more than they did, but watching them going up the famous steps only made me feel even more removed from the occasion.

That night the Liverpool boys went to Planet Hollywood. I went as Razor, trying to gee-up the other lads – 'Come on!

Who gives a fuck? It's just another game.' I stood at the bar slapping people on the back when inside I felt worse than I ever had in my entire life. Totally broken. Later, me and Stan Collymore wandered out to Piccadilly Circus. I dared Stan to put my jacket on the statue of Eros. Stan being Stan, he climbed 10 metres and hung it on the angel at the top. For once, with Eros there was no love lost.

While dumping that loser's jacket felt good, the only thing that ever came near to anaesthetising the hurt for me after that Cup Final embarrassment and humiliation was booze. Looking back, that was a big moment. The link in my head was made – alcohol takes the pain away. That 'knowledge' would come back to haunt me. When I was lost and hurting in retirement, there was only one place I was ever going to look.

For now, I had other issues to deal with. After being overlooked, my confidence took a massive knock. My default position was to blame it all on myself – I'm not good enough. No-one thinks I can do it anymore. Managers don't believe in me. That was the beginning of the end. That's when my discipline went. Drink more. Eat what I want. Train less. I was never the same person on or off the pitch after that. And by that I mean mentally and physically. If mentally you're not with it, that's when your fitness drops, which is when you pick up more injuries, which in itself is when your standard of performance begins to slip. All of a sudden, sport, the thing you have relied on all your life to deliver the good times, is doing exactly the opposite. The Cup Final was the start of a spiral which never ended. The start of mad, bad, sad, glad syndrome. Until that day I had never ever doubted myself. Never. Not once. Now it was all I did. Anxiety bubbled underneath. I was gone – a volcano waiting to erupt.

Back then, the FA Cup was the last game of the season, just as it should be. On the Sunday, the lads disappeared in different directions. My direction was madness. I spent that six-week break getting pissed and eating anything I felt like. One thought went round and round in my head – 'What's the fucking point?'

When I reported back for training, the hurt and frustration was still coursing round my system. Everyone could see how disappointed I was. Dougie Livermore, my old coach at Tottenham, who I'd known since I was 17, and who was at Liverpool at the time, didn't know what to say – I think he was embarrassed that the club had treated me so unfairly. Roy Evans could also see how pissed off I was. To make me feel better, he told me he'd made a mistake. It was the last thing I wanted to hear. I would rather he'd tried to justify it than say he was wrong. It doesn't make you feel better to know you missed out on the biggest occasion of your life because some-one made a mistake. There was no reason I hadn't played in the FA Cup Final, the only game I'd have walked to the end of the Earth to play in, other than 'it was a mistake'?

I want to be clear here, I don't blame Roy Evans. I loved Roy and actually went on to become his assistant manager at Swindon Town. The FA Cup Final team was his call. He did what he thought was right in the way he thought was right. Roy Evans didn't ruin my career. I ruined my career because I didn't know how to cope and there was no-one to share my mental anguish. That's what was missing in all this – sharing. There was no-one to speak to. No-one to put an arm round me and say, 'Come on, mate, you can get past this. It'll be all right in the end.' At the very least I should have had a bust-up with the gaffer and got it out of my system, which might also have forced him to explain his decision, and that would have given me something to think about. I'd seen other players have that big blast of emotion and move on. One time we'd played away at Ipswich and Jan Molby hadn't got a game. He was absolutely steaming. He went up to Roy. 'Why didn't you pick me?', he asked in that weird Scouse-Danish accent. Roy mumbled something about formations, tactics, that kind of stuff. 'You picked that c***,' he said, indicating Phil Babb, 'and paid five million quid for him. Instead of being stuck here we could have flown home on a fucking jet!'

But I internalised my pain. I built a wall round myself and didn't let anyone in. I didn't want anyone to see just how badly being dropped had bothered me. I was going right back to what I'd always been taught at Millwall – 'Never let anyone know when you're hurt – it's a sign of weakness.' It didn't matter what form that hurt took, emotional or physical, all that mattered was no-one knew you were feeling it. That was football. At West Ham, when I fractured my eye socket in a collision with the Wimbledon striker Carl Leaburn and was wondering at half-time whether to carry on, Harry Red-knapp asked me if I was a man or a mouse. I'm not putting that on Harry. I was asking myself the same question on the inside – and I'd already decided I was a man. I was thinking of Terry Butcher, not him off *Tom & Jerry*. Taking a physical hammering was all part of Razor's big macho world. If I had a cut, I'd squeeze and tear at it to create more blood. I'd have loved to have the claret streaming through a head bandage and down my shirt like Terry did in one of the best footballing photos of all time. Get this, I was so attached to this idea of being and looking hard that after one cut I asked the doctor to stick in eleven stitches to beat my previous record of ten. He actually did it as well. I was great with the physical stuff. The mental? There was no way of getting it out of my system. I was clever in my own way but, like most people, that didn't extend to understanding what was happening in my head. In a pit of despair at Liverpool, I needed to talk to someone who, unlike me and everyone else at the club, could unravel my thoughts and knit them back together in a pattern that made sense to me – that gave me something to work with for the future. But I never had that outlet, and so instead just wanted to be on my own.

The way I saw it, I'd done everything right in my career – trained, looked after myself, exercised – to get me to a position where I could play in the biggest game of the lot, only for it all to come tumbling down on top of me. I'd been flying, had the best life in the world, and then crashed down into the mud. My family would try to help by telling me it was the manager's fault – he was an idiot for leaving me out. But I never heard those words. I just thought it was me. How else do you explain it when you haven't put a foot wrong week after week after week? Confidence is a skill. You can teach anyone to be stronger, quicker, cleverer, better tactically, more aware, but if they're not confident then none of it will work like it should. And that's what happened to me. I had another year-and-a-half at Liverpool and that confidence vacuum was never filled. I even took it with me when I moved on from Liverpool to West Ham. Whereas before I'd totally backed myself, now I'd run onto the pitch thinking, 'Please don't let me have a nightmare.' I constantly feared making a mess of things that I'd done a thousand times without the slightest element of doubt.

Missing the Cup Final had become an ogre in my mind. It wasn't like I could just brush it off and say, 'Oh well, there's always next year.' The odds are stacked against you ever getting that far again. In 1996, aged 28, I was at my physical peak. The chances of me ever making it to Wembley again were only going to decrease hugely year by year from then on. And in the end I didn't. The only other time I got proper close to the Final was the semi-final defeat against Arsenal in 1993 when I was at Tottenham. But I was younger then and returning to Wembley still felt like a real possibility. And at least I'd played in that game. I couldn't beat myself up on that front. I'd also played in a League Cup Final for Liverpool and been on the winning team, but in my heart that was never the same as an FA Cup Final. I'd played at Wembley for Southampton in the final of the catchily-named Zenith Data Systems Cup, the competition created to fill a gap after English clubs were banned from Europe, but it was all a bit Mickey Mouse compared to the real deal.

The first six months especially after the Cup Final, I was lost. I got myself into a mental mess that I couldn't get out of. There was something else about being dropped. It was the first time I'd failed. And I had no idea how to deal with it. Again, alcohol seemed as good an answer as any. Before the Cup Final I was drinking for fun. Now I was drinking for the fuck of it. I've heard people talk about losing their mojo. I don't know what a mojo is or if I ever had one in the first place, but if I did it was definitely gone. I was in and around the England set-up at that time but told the manager Terry Venables I wanted to take a step away. Mentally I wasn't interested – because never again in my life did I want to have that feeling of disappointment, of being part of something only for it to be snatched away. If I joined up with England and then never made the squad, I was setting myself up to fail again; to experience another massive low. As a professional footballer I'd been set up to succeed, not to fail. I don't mean losing the odd fixture here and there – that's part and parcel of the game. But to fail in the big moments, by not even getting in the team, that was something I couldn't handle. I was Razor, top man, the life and soul. I turned up and made a difference. To do anything else wasn't part of the deal I'd made with myself as either a sportsman or a human being. I couldn't handle the thought of turning up – and then being turned away again.

Hard to believe, really. Everything had been so sweet in my life to that point, and then BANG!, with one short sentence, 'Sorry, Razor . . .', it had all turned so sour.

2

BLESS 'IM

Neil Ruddock was born in St George's Hospital, Wandsworth. Razor Ruddock evolved among the pitches and pubs of south London and Kent.

I spent my very early years in a council flat in Tooting before, like a lot of London families in the late sixties, my mum and dad were tempted by the promise of a better life out east. By some distance I was the youngest of three – my brothers Colin and Gary are five and nine years older than me. My guess is I popped up as an unexpected guest. Maybe Mum and Dad had a couple too many drinks one night at Butlin's. Actually, more likely Pontins. I was giving it the big 'un there with Butlin's! Very occasionally, if Dad had a bonus at work, we did sometimes go abroad – to a holiday camp in Wales. Anyway, whatever the circumstances of my conception, I was definitely the baby by comparison – and by far the favourite. I don't even have to worry about what my brothers might think about me saying that – because they agree. Mum used to call me her 'little soldier'. So often did she use the phrase 'Bless 'im!' that even now my brothers take the piss by saying it to me. Go round to Mum's house and there's pictures of me all round her front room. Gary's in the hallway and Colin's in the toilet.

When I got a bit older, Mum would give me steak if I was playing football the next day. My brothers would get a tin of Spam between them. Alternatively, I'd have a lovely tuna and mayo sandwich while they had cucumber and vinegar. To get their own back they'd burp all over my food when Mum wasn't looking. Nearly half a century on and they still hold the grudge, even if when I say 'steak', I mean a minute steak, the smallest, thinnest cut out there. We never had proper steak. But minute steak was good enough for me, and it seemed to do the trick when I ran out on to the pitch.

While I'm still a bit nervous ordering a steak in a restaurant now, waiting for one of my brothers to appear from under the table and belch on it, I should really thank them for their undying ability to be a pain in the arse. While admittedly Gary did used to shit me up by telling me, 'I'm not your brother, I'm a ghost,' when 'looking after me' while Mum was out earning a wage, at that point picking potatoes in the fields. When you have two older brothers it's kind of inevitable you're going to have to be a bit noisier, a bit louder, to get noticed. You soon learn to fight to be heard. We actually used to have boxing nights in the house. 'Push the settee back – mind the fire!' Mum and Dad would even invite their friends round to watch. Because of the size difference, my brothers would fight me on their knees. I might have been the smallest but I didn't hold back. I smacked my brother Colin so hard one time that it drew blood. 'Go on, do that again!' he goaded me. So I did. Mum and Dad nearly died laughing. That's definitely where that combative, competitive, side of me came from. It's just that it's lasted another fifty years.

I got it from my mum too. She was a south London girl, fiery. Like the rest of her generation, she'd lived through the war, staying in London with her mum, while my dad, on the other hand, was evacuated to Wales, the woman who looked after him left heartbroken when she had to give him back – later in life me and Dad would drive up there so they could be reunited. Stories like that make you think how hard those times were in terms of the emotional bonds that were formed only to be ripped apart. The war didn't just end in 1945 and everything was sweet again. The sacrifices those people made went on for years and years. You had to be tough, and

Mum was exactly that. She never lost that fighting edge. If anyone gave her grief, she'd let them know about it. If she bought me a shirt and it ripped after a couple of days, she'd be straight back down the shop. She literally wouldn't move until the money was back in her hand. And she was right. She'd worked hard for that shirt. Why should she let someone have the money out of her purse for something that was a load of garbage? After the potato-picking, she worked at a branch of a frozen food store. Every time the manager went out we'd get a phone call from her – 'Quick! Bring the car!' We'd jump in and race round to the back of the shop. There'd be all sorts flying out – joints of meat, pies, the lot. It was like doing a bank job. We had to buy a chest freezer to stick it all in. She didn't feel too bad about it because she'd been round to the manager's house one day and clocked that he had a chest freezer full of the stuff too – 'Well, if he's doing it, I'm having a bit!'

Mum's battling spirit meant she was a good netball player when she was younger. She had a lot of potential – until the day she turned round and belted an opponent with a right-hander and was banned for six months. One time me and her were watching Gary in a cup final and as the linesman ran past he gave me a shove and sent me flying. That was it, she was off down the line after him. He was lucky not to see out the rest of that game with his flag flapping out of his arse. Years later I did a sliding tackle on a player on the line, went straight under him, and took out a liner instead. On YouTube you can still see me do a celebratory air punch as I trot away. That was for you, Mum!

If Mum was competitive, then having three boys all playing sport only made her more so. You didn't mess with her or her family. If anyone did, she wasn't just going to stand back and let it go. She got that from her own mum, who really was as tough as old boots. Misbehave with Mum and you could expect to feel the sharp thwack of a spoon on the back of the leg, or the well-worn threat of telling Dad when he got home. Dad didn't have to say anything to scare us. He just gave us his special stare. I still get goosebumps thinking about it, in particular when Gary drew a moustache on his passport and made him look like El Chapo. Bad, bad, idea. Mum's authority changed a bit when we got older. If she said she was going to tell Dad what we'd been up to, we'd lift her up and put her in the sink until she promised not to say anything. Either that or lock her outside.

Dad, while also a big character, was slightly less feisty than Mum. Had Dad seen her pursue that linesman he'd have been embarrassed to death. Dad was more of a cheeky chappie than anything else. He looked like Cooperman, the Russ Abbot character, or, more preferably for him, Georgie Best, and everyone loved him. Unlike me, though, he wasn't a big drinker – three pints and he was pissed. Mum used to drink more than him, although her ability to get confused has never been alcohol-related. The other week I told her I was going to Silverstone. 'Got any tips?' she asked. She thought it was a horse-racing track. 'Yes, Mum. I know one that does 250 miles an hour down the home straight.'

Dad was a Fulham fan. He had trials for the Cottagers but then National Service came along and got in the way. Maybe I'd have followed him and been a Fulham fan too, but instead I was told by my brothers that I was Millwall, despite the fact that, living round Tooting, the nearest teams were actually Fulham and Chelsea. But they were north of the river and if you're born south London, you stay south London. My brothers were steeped in Millwall tradition by the time we moved out to Ashford. Not even being two at that point, when they told me I was Millwall I didn't have much say in the matter.

Ashford became our new home after the shopfitters Dad worked for in Balham moved out there. The workforce went with them, the town soon becoming known as 'Little London' so numerous were the people and companies from the capital setting up. Dad was a talented bloke. He repaired a cross on Coventry Cathedral and made the fireguard for the *Royal Yacht Britannia* – which in my book makes us regal. His speciality was banks, bulletproof glass and all that kind of stuff. People would sometimes ask what he did for a living. 'I do banks!' he'd say breezily, just to see the look on their faces. Moving to Ashford was the best thing they could have ever done for us. We grew up loving the freedom of being able to play out all day in the woods. It shows how new it all was to us that Gary rushed home one day to tell Mum he'd seen a load of poodles in a field. She calmly pointed out that what he'd actually seen were lambs. For her part, Mum was pleased because we were going to get a bathroom: a bath, a sink, a toilet that no-one else had ever used.

Doubtless if I hadn't gone into football I'd have become an apprentice and done the same as Dad. As it was, my apprenticeship was served on the football pitch. While I didn't realise it at the time, having older brothers was a great route into a career in football. It meant I was playing with lads much bigger and older than me from the start. Constantly fighting to bridge that age gap, it was inevitable I'd improve quicker than most. My brothers recall that virtually from the start I had people literally chasing shadows. I could do keepie-uppies with a golf ball, all kind of tricks. The only thing that let me down, they say, is that I used to wear my shorts hitched up too high. Then again, neither of them has ever understood fashion.

Then there was the physicality. In that sort of company, you didn't cry when you got hurt. And having my brothers on hand meant I could kick the opposition. My feet were especially well-suited for that purpose. As a young lad I'd been told that pissing on them makes the skin harder. And so that's what I did. I'm not sure if it worked. I think what really happens is you just have a player on the pitch who constantly stinks of piss.

My brothers weren't overly protective of me but would 100 per cent step in if someone was giving me a bit of grief. Both could handle themselves. Gary, the brains of the outfit, went to the grammar school, announcing his arrival by decking the headmaster's son on the first day. Colin, meanwhile, knocked three geezers out while playing football and got banned for a year.

It was definitely a case of one minute looking after me and the next wanting to kill me. One time when my brothers were in charge, I disappeared. There was panic all-round. They had the neighbours out searching for me and everything. People were convinced I'd been taken. I knew all this because I had the perfect view of it happening. Those houses had been built with carports, and I was lying flat on the roof of ours watching the best drama I'd seen in months. In the end I got bored with being missing. When my mum walked underneath, I went 'Boo!' The best thing about it was my brothers got told off for not looking after me.

Then there was the Cake Cup, a tradition at our school whereby every class would play in a knock-out football tournament, the winner receiving one of Mr Kipling's finest. The competition had a handicap system meaning the younger lads had a chance of winning against the older boys. When my class played Colin's, the handicap meant they had to beat us by twenty-four goals. That's a lot, especially in a game that's twelve minutes each way, but they were a good few years older than us and they'd still have done it easy – were it not for a cunning plan hatched by our form teacher. Instead of trying to beat them at football, every time we got hold of the ball we booted it off the pitch and down a massive slope. With no time added on, a huge amount of the game was wasted as my brother's side huffed, puffed and swore their way back and forth to fetch the ball. It worked a treat – well, just. They were

23–0 up when the final whistle went. I still see it as one of the greatest examples of tactical genius in footballing history.

Cake Cup aside, any natural talent was always going to blossom playing alongside older kids which is why I was picked up by Millwall at 12, although I looked much older than my age. I'd see opposition managers looking me up and down – 'Come off it. He's about six foot tall. He must be a ringer. Let's see his cards!' John Fashanu was the same, only the ageing never stopped. By the time he was 20, he looked about 35. Being noticed at such a young age didn't go to my head. Even if I'd wanted to, no-one around me would have allowed it to happen. If I'd have started playing Charlie Big Bollocks, my brothers would soon have brought me crashing back down to earth with a clip round the earhole.

And it wasn't like I was the only one with a bit of talent. Gary could probably have made it as a pro, but he got side-tracked, like most blokes, by drink and girls. Football got in the way! He remains the intellectual one. He's even got a bookcase – which came in handy when we were up at his house one night and he ran out of coal. He went out the room for a minute and Colin chucked the thickest book he could find on the flames. Gary wasn't best pleased. It was Nelson Mandela's autobiography and he was about fifteen pages from the end. The good news is he can now fill that gap in his collection with a book by his brother.

Living out in Kent, I might never have been spotted by Millwall were it not for a mate who played for a Sunday team in south-east London called St Thomas More, basically a Millwall youth team from Welling, playing at the old Royal Herbert Hospital in Shooters Hill, an amazing set of buildings with a football pitch right in the middle. From the start I loved St Thomas More, and it felt like they loved me. After we won the London Cup competition the league changed the rules so that players had to live within 15 miles of the team's base. St Thomas More responded not by getting rid of me, but by moving to a different league with different rules so I could still play.

It was with St Thomas More that I first began to see how with football I could not only live my dream but see the world. When I was 14, Dad went with me to America so I could play in the Dallas Cup, a prestigious international youth soccer tournament. Via endless fetes and collections, St Thomas More had managed to raise the money to go. We played teams from all over the world, before eventually getting beaten by the home side, the Texas Longhorns, in the final.

As if the football wasn't exciting enough, we visited Southfork, famed home of the Ewings in *Dallas*, the biggest show on TV at the time. Considering the oil money in the game now, it's sad that JR never thought to invest in Millwall. He'd have looked good wandering round Bermondsey in a Stetson. We also visited the Texas Book Depository from where Lee Harvey Oswald supposedly killed John F. Kennedy. I say 'supposedly' because there's no way he could have shot twice from that position in the time the president's car took to pass (I'll present my theories in my next book). When we went to see the city's football club, Dallas Tornado, we were astonished to find they actually had an organist playing during the game. When Tornado were on the attack he played at a really high tempo, like a chase in an old Keystone Cops film. When they were defending he slowed right down and played something like you'd hear at a funeral. I was absolutely wetting myself laughing. Rounding off the trip was a mad week at a cowboy ranch in San Antonio, riding horses, fishing, all sorts of stuff. The whole thing was amazing. At that time, I didn't know anyone who'd been on an aeroplane. The furthest I'd been was Skegness. Now here I was in the States having the time of my life. I couldn't help thinking about the rather less glamorous 'character-building' school trips I'd avoided because of football commitments. Colin and a couple of mates had once been dumped on a sandbank off Llanelli with a couple of oil drums and some old telegraph poles and told to build a raft and make their way back to shore. They were halfway to Northern Ireland when they were picked up by a passing boat. Back on dry land, I was having a great time kicking a ball around.

After a while, Dad started working in Saudi, the money he earned taking us from a council estate to Sandyhurst Lane, which is still the number one address in Ashford. Our diet changed too – liver suddenly appeared. Dad's job had a heavy influence on our house. Our front door was effectively a bank's, so heavy you needed to be Arnold Schwarzenegger to open it, and all the windows were made of bulletproof glass. A couple of decades later and it would have been a shoo-in for *Grand Designs*. Eventually, Dad moved out to Saudi full-time. By then I was 16. My life was football, football, football. I clearly had a future with Millwall, and had two older brothers to look out for me, so Mum felt comfortable joining Dad out in Saudi. I went out with them for a couple of weeks, but then when the time came for me to return to England I couldn't face it. Going back alone and starting out on a whole new unknown chapter without them felt totally overwhelming. My parents could see the state I was in and so Dad told Millwall there was a problem with my visa. I missed two weeks of pre-season before finally accepting I had to get back on the plane.

Back home, football kept me busy but I missed Mum and Dad massively. Emotionally, there was a huge gap in my life. For anyone, having a mum and dad around every day and for them to disappear from your life is going to take a bit of getting used to. For years I'd also been totally reliant on Dad for my football. He used to take me everywhere. We couldn't always afford it, but somehow he'd find the five quid it cost in petrol to get me to training every week and the three quid it cost for a game. Millwall used to train at Catford and Dad would run me over in his mustard Austin Allegro. We were halfway back to Ashford one night when he turned to me in the passenger seat – 'This ain't our car!'

'What do you mean?'

'Look at those sunglasses. They ain't mine.'

He was right – this definitely wasn't our car. For a start, it smelt nice. It hadn't had a pair of my sweaty football socks festering on the back seat for a week. We did a quick U-turn, parked up, slipped into our own mustard Allegro, and went home. Things happened when Dad was around and I loved him and looked up to him massively. Sometimes he'd pick up hitchhikers just to liven up the journey. We'd only be able to take them five minutes up the road but it made us laugh. He was the sort of bloke who was always great company – clever, funny, lively mind.

Once he'd gone to Saudi, my lifts disappeared with him, which meant moving to east London, Barking way, and into the home of the mum and dad of Millwall youth coach Roger Cross. There was me and Gary Middleton from Newcastle, known as Tiddles – the kind of nickname that never came my way. To be fair, unlike me, Gary was soft and cuddly. Rumour was he also had a very rough tongue.

Losing that connection, not just to Mum and Dad, but also my brothers who were working all hours and so physically couldn't look out for me as much they'd liked to have done, meant I began living a separate life, and it maybe had more of an effect on me than I've ever fully realised. Up to that point, we'd been a close family, but now, in a flash, it had all gone. I wasn't the sort to dwell on stuff, but I knew I didn't like that feeling of being on my own, and, for better or worse, I'd avoid it in the years to come.

The flipside of this sudden change in circumstances was that I grew up quickly, and if you want to be a footballer that's no bad thing. Professional sport is hard. You need to be tough. Makes sense then that the quicker someone grows up, the quicker they'll be a good footballer. Dad saw this new improved side to me when, aged 16, I made my England youth debut against Ireland at Leeds. I had no idea he was coming until I stepped off the coach and there he was, having specially made the trip back to England. No way was he going to miss a landmark like that. Mum, on the other hand, never came to games. She loved football but used to get too nervous, thinking I might get hurt. She did come to Anfield once and was utterly broken up when she heard the crowd singing 'You'll Never Walk Alone'. Then, once the whistle blew, she didn't watch the game. She did nothing but stare at me. I looked up at her in the crowd a few times and there she was, looking straight back at me.

While Mum was way too anxious to come to my games, once Dad came back from Saudi after four years in the sun he would follow me everywhere, often with his own dad Percy – actually he was called Keith, but in our world no-one ever seemed to be called by their real name. Dad would travel to all sorts of far-flung and exotic places across Europe, and Sunderland. He never said out loud that he was proud of me, but whenever he said to me, 'Do your best', there was a look in his eye that told me he was. None of it would have happened without him. Yes, because of the endless running me around, but also because of one of the greatest bits of advice I was ever given. When I was a young teenager, Dad told me that whenever a scout or a coach came up to me and asked what I wanted to do in football, win the FA Cup or whatever, I should just say, 'I want to try and do my best every time I play football.' That would tell them everything they wanted to know. 'Scouts don't want dreams,' Dad told me, 'they want effort.'

The only place Dad wouldn't watch me was Chelsea, because if Fulham weren't the away side he wouldn't entertain going there. As he put it, 'Chelsea is a little team in Fulham.' He could be proper old-school like that. Fortunately, he had no issue with Millwall, and was more than happy that I was thriving with the Lions, as was I, although if I'm honest the team I really worshipped as a kid was Liverpool – the likes of Tommy Smith, Jimmy Case, Emlyn Hughes and of course Kevin Keegan. I had posters of Keegan on my bedroom walls. I'd have had them on the ceiling as well if I could. People say, 'Hang on, you were a Millwall fan!', but *Shoot!* and *Match!* magazines wouldn't really have posters of Millwall players. Who'd want a giant picture of Brian Horne on their wall? So besotted with Keegan was I that, while writing this chapter, a poem I haven't heard for forty years just popped into my head:

He came to Anfield in '71,
Shy, embarrassed, a coalminer's son.
Though his signing was hardly a major event,
the money turned out to be more than well spent.
Courage, agility, coupled with speed,
Kevin Keegan was born to succeed.

Kevin's Liverpool strike partner John Toshack wrote that. It might sound mad carrying those words around for decades, but the thing is everything was football for me as a kid. All I ever talked about, all I ever did. In the holidays, I was that classic kid – out at nine in the morning, back at five at night, playing football the whole time. There wasn't anything else. Computers weren't a thing back then. I wonder what that kid would have thought if he'd known that a few years later Kevin Keegan would actually want to sign him – a proposal that was scuppered by Newcastle United then being in the Second Division. Had they been in the top flight it might have been different.

I didn't just admire Kevin as a footballer, I wanted to copy everything about him. I even had a Kevin Keegan perm when he left Liverpool for Hamburg. The reaction could have been worse, maybe because by then I was in Kent, not south London. After the perm I went for streaks and then a little ponytail like a New Romantic. I was also a Mod for a while – it was cheaper clobber than the New Romantics. I've been through a few phases in my life and perhaps the ponytail was the most extreme. In the end my dad made me cut it off. There was a lot he didn't like about it, but especially the little red bow I put in it. That was a brave move at the time. Looking like Little Miss Muffet was the sort of thing that could attract a fair bit of negative attention. Even with the protection of two big brothers I never went to Millwall with the bow in. Such a look probably wouldn't have been advisable anywhere in those days, but especially not at Cold Blow Lane. This was, after all, a place where they'd confiscate the laces from your boots before you went in. That way you couldn't run, and if you couldn't run, you couldn't fight. On the way out you'd grab a couple from the basket. Everyone would walk home with the wrong laces. You'd end up with one red and one yellow.

By the way, the emphasis in Millwall is on the 'wall' not the 'mill'. You can always tell a true Millwall fan like that. Not that there's been many hangers-on down the years. It's not that sort of club. But the intimidating atmosphere that

Millwall was infamous for was one of the main reasons I loved going as a kid. Walking through the old arches on the approach to Cold Blow Lane, the smell of hamburgers in the air, the shouting and the chanting, was so exciting. And then into the ground itself, a proper bearpit, concrete terraces and metal railings. The tunnel was on wheels and would extend 30 yards onto the pitch to save the away team from the crowd's hostility – and the same for the home team if we lost. Back then you could actually walk around most of the ground and make sure you were towards whatever end Millwall were attacking. And of course, best of all, being on Millwall's books as a schoolboy meant I got free tickets.

Whenever Millwall is mentioned, the word 'hooliganism' is never far away. The mid-eighties was a particularly tasty time, which as a kid just added to the exhilaration. I'll be honest, to watch big groups of lads – and actually grown men – going at each other was so thrilling. Myself, I was always more of a spectator when it came to matchday violence. It's no secret that I was at Luton in 1985 for the most infamous Millwall match of the lot. The sixth round FA Cup tie is remembered for what happened on the pitch – but unfortunately not for anything the players were involved with. The riot that happened that night felt inevitable before the game had even kicked off. Bricks and bottles had been hurled at the Millwall fans as they made their way to the ground. That continued when they actually got inside, with stones being lobbed from outside into the away section. The atmosphere just got grimmer and grimmer as kick-off approached. It was reckoned double Millwall's usual home attendance travelled to the match and by the end, especially with us losing 1–0, it was obvious there was going to be a pitch invasion, although even then I don't think anyone expected the sheer scale of it. Seats were ripped out and hurled as hundreds streamed onto the pitch. The police retreated before coming back with a baton charge. It was mayhem – and I was right there on the grass with everyone else. I had no choice – when that invasion happened, the momentum of all those hundreds of people carried you out there whether you liked it or not. There was me and my fellow Millwall first-year apprentice Mickey Marks, who would later become the youngest Mill-wall player to score a hat-trick. All we wanted to do was get the hell out of there, especially when the police dogs appeared, a bunch of snarling Alsatians who definitely weren't going to be pacified with a tickle behind the ear. It must have been just as we were legging it that the photographer for the *South London Press* newspaper took the picture that would fill the front page of the next edition – me and Mickey with HOOLIGANS! in giant letters underneath. It wasn't quite what either of us had planned with regards to our climb up the footballing career ladder and Millwall boss George Graham clearly felt the same. When the paper landed on his desk, his reaction was heard in Australia. The list of people we'd let down ran the length of a telephone directory. Me and Mickey spent the next two weeks with a brush in our hands sweeping the terraces. It could have been worse – we might have been arrested. The police kept the Millwall fans in at the end, presumably to nick a good few of them, but one of my cousins climbed a floodlight and somehow managed to get down and unlock the gates. A horrible night, and one which confirmed Millwall fans as public enemy number one. 'No-one likes us, we don't care,' and all that.

George's rage at my involvement was the first thing I thought about a few months later when I borrowed a pair of Gary's jeans only for a lump of marijuana to fall out the pocket. Can you imagine if that had happened in front of George? I'd have been out on my arse and maybe blacklisted from ever playing again. Thanks to Gary, my football career could have been over before it had even started. He really should have looked after that stuff better. Another time our

Jack Russell ate his stash. The poor sod didn't come down off the ceiling for days.

While pushing a broom round Cold Blow Lane wasn't quite what I had in mind as a footballer, I'd done worse. As an apprentice my job was to clean the home dressing room toilets. Slightly less awful was cleaning the first-team players' boots. At Millwall that included deadly defender Alan Walker. I actually still see Alan once a week and he still scares the life out of me. I'm still offering to clean his shoes now – when I became an apprentice at Millwall I hadn't realised it would last forty years. For all the horror of venturing into a dressing room toilet with a pair of Marigolds and a bog brush, it does give you discipline and respect for the older players. In fact, compared to a lot of kids, I actually had a lot of discipline in my life. My drinking, for instance, only really started in earnest when I became a pro. That was what they did and I wanted to fit in with them. As an apprentice, fitting in with the pros wasn't a thing – I'd have to knock on the dressing room door before I went in. Chances are I'd barely have taken a step inside before I was dispatched to get someone a cup of tea. I'm not saying I liked doing it, same as I didn't like cleaning the toilets, but I understood why it was happening and what the club was trying to teach me.

Thankfully, these things do come full circle. You might have heard of the lad who cleaned my boots at Liverpool – Steven Gerrard. I actually saw him a few years ago at his testimonial dinner and afterwards he came over to me at the bar and gave me a few quid – 'treat your kids'. Initially, I didn't twig, but then he reminded me that when he cleaned my boots I'd given him a hundred pound bonus at Christmas. He'd never forgotten it. By the time Stevie G was cleaning my boots, a hundred quid was neither here nor there. But in all honesty, while the money side of the game makes a lot of headlines, when you start out it's the last thing on your mind. Like most kids, at 17 I was happy just to have signed a professional contract. As the more established players would tell me, when you get older, and can play consistently to a good level, and have proven your ability, that's when you get the money.

The following season, with just a handful of Freight Rover Trophy appearances under my belt, George called me into his office. It was transfer deadline day. 'You've got an hour,' he told me. 'You need to make up your mind whether to go to Norwich or Tottenham.' What was I supposed to do? Mum and Dad were still in Saudi and my brothers could have been anywhere. Even if I had known where they were, there were no mobile phones anyway. Luckily, I did somehow manage to contact my dad. He wanted to know from George what it was all about, why he was getting rid of me – 'Isn't he good enough?' Of course, the truth was the exact opposite, and at a club like Millwall George couldn't turn down the chance of bringing in fifty-five grand for a 17-year-old. While I was shocked and confused, I soon came to the conclusion that Norwich wasn't an option. While there was a good chance of first-team football at Carrow Road, I was ambitious and wasn't sure it was a move that would take me in the direction I wanted. There was a chance I could spend years out east and just fall off the map. Spurs, on the other hand, were one of the biggest clubs in the country, a glamour side with an incredible history and the trophies to go with it. Not to mention that fantastic kit. I'd actually made my debut for Millwall reserves at White Hart Lane, against a Spurs team containing no less than their megastar strikers Garth Crooks and Steve Archibald. I was still at school and so playing at that famous stadium I'd seen so many times on the telly was something really special. The dressing room not only had a huge team bath but a heated floor. Just magnificent.

There was still the little matter of my wages to sort out. With no-one else to help with the deal, George effectively became my first agent. When we turned up at White Hart Lane to meet Spurs boss Peter Shreeves, I was delighted to hear he was offering £275 a week. Fantastic! Where do I sign? George, on the other hand, didn't look quite so happy. In fact, he looked like he'd been slapped round the face with a wet haddock.

'Right, come on!' he told me, 'we're off to Norwich.'

'What? Why? What's happening?' He was literally dragging me out the door into the corridor.

'Hang on!' Shreeves was panicking. 'Come back!'

I quickly twigged what George was up to. This was the football version of haggling over a second-hand motor. George didn't want me to be a doormat. Thanks to him I walked out of that meeting with £340 a week and a brand new Ford Escort XR3. I felt like I was flying. I even treated myself to a top from Benetton – at forty quid, the most expensive shirt I'd ever bought. In no time, Gary nicked it and went to work in it. Back it came, covered in filler. This was what I had to put up with. I grew up around people who just didn't understand a bit of class!

While £55k and an XR3 was a lot of money for a 17-year-old, it should be remembered that at that point I was already turning out for England Under-18s. I was, in my opinion, the best kid in London. I wasn't just a blood and bollocks defender, I'd been a winger and centre-forward for years. I could play football – and Tottenham were a footballing team. What was a little more unpredictable was my behaviour.

My brothers had shown me early in life that you don't necessarily need to follow the rules. When I was 15, they used to take me to the pub – so I could drive them home. We were actually pulled over by the Old Bill one night. The constable had just got his notebook out when he realised he didn't have anything to write with. 'Er, any of you lads got a pen?' 'Terribly sorry, officer, but no.' He had no choice but to let us go. The fact it was blowing a gale and pissing down with rain probably helped. I'm not too sure what would have happened if we had been nicked. What's the defence for a 15-year-old driving his two pissed brothers home from the pub in the dark? Ironic, really, that Colin would go on to join the Force. Me and Gary would occasionally see him on duty – 'You'll never take us alive, copper!' we'd shout and run off, shoppers wondering what the bleeding hell was going on. Another time, Colin thought all his Christmases had come at once when he was posted at a Millwall home game. He had visions of spending many a Saturday afternoon getting paid to watch the team he loved. Sadly, it was to be a one-off. Colin jumped up and cheered when the home team scored, got suitably bollocked by the sergeant, and was never asked again.

While as my brothers' designated driver I'd always be sober, I'd actually started drinking a year before the close shave with the traffic cop. I'd drink stuff that had been left around the house. We had a bar that was shaped like the front of a boat – fantastic, little lights on it and everything. Dad used to let me drink shandies. When I was with my brothers it was cans of Mackeson stout. 'Makes you strong,' they'd say. 'Full of iron. Good for a young footballer.'

Drinking was very much in the family. My Uncle Bill's house was more like a pub. Sweep aside the strips on the door that kept the flies out and there it was – booze heaven. I can still remember that smell of whisky – lovely. But The Fox in Ashford was our usual haunt. All three of us Ruddock brothers turned out for the pub football team, which stuck out in the league for always playing in a full Liverpool kit, which was bad news for the lad who was a Man United fan. Every game he'd try to cover up the badge with black tape. Managing The Fox, Jimmy Kelly became my first ever gaffer. Later, when I was at Tottenham, I was asked to do a questionnaire for the *Daily Star* – different player, same questions every week. When it came to 'favourite manager' I put 'Jimmy Kelly'.

All day, Jimmy was getting phone calls from people wanting to know who he was and what he'd done for Neil Ruddock. I don't think I took that questionnaire as seriously as some people. 'What does your dad do?' Property owner in Knightsbridge. 'Your brother?' Nuclear scientist. It went on and on. The Fox always held fond memories, to the extent that me, my brothers and a few others who used to drink there as kids bought it when it looked like it was going to be turned into flats. Not long after, six lads walked through the door effing and blinding. My brother was having none of it. 'Oi! What do you think you're doing, coming in here swearing like that?' I gave him a gentle nudge – 'If you remember, we were ten times worse.' I nipped to the toilet, came back and he was sat there joining in!

I didn't let the little matter of school get in the way of drinking. At dinnertime a couple of us used to head to the local. We'd spend our dinner money on a bitter top – not the best drink but the cheapest there was. We'd actually stand at the bar in our school uniforms. There was no problem getting served – the landlord knew my brothers. I loved that buzz of getting away with something, a feeling which would go with me through life. I got that same little bit of excitement when at the same age I'd have a drink on matchdays at Millwall.

They used to sell a Swiss beer called Hürlimann's in the ground, like Stella Artois but on steroids. We used to call it Hooligans. I was far from the only one out on the piss at that age. Half the kids I knew were doing the same. Nowadays it's changed. Drinking has gone out of fashion. Kids prefer to smoke a bit of weed. Maybe it's for the best. Less messy. The first time I ever got proper pissed was on that eighties classic, Pernod and black. My mum actually thought I'd cut my feet open when in reality I'd just walked through my own sick. That aniseed smell of Pernod has made me want to throw up ever since. I was reminded of my dinnertime drinking when I got to Spurs and met their midfielder, David Howells. That bloke had hollow legs. Lunchtimes, we'd go to TGI Fridays and get smashed. Only Monday, Tuesday, Wednesday, mind. Never Thursday and Friday before a game on Saturday. That would have been out of order.

Believe it or not I had been quite shy when I was proper little. But first playing football and then going down the pub with my brothers soon put paid to that. You couldn't be a wallflower in that environment. Being around people so much older and more experienced than me meant I was a man at 17, in football terms at least. On the pitch there was no tricky transition into men's football. It was seamless – I'd been getting quicker and stronger and harder for years. And I wasn't afraid to get stuck in and tackle someone, whoever they were, whatever their reputation. Off the pitch, meanwhile, I'd learned how to make myself heard in adult company – loud adult company! Slowly but surely, the character that would become Razor was emerging. It felt like being this person – everyone's mate, constant fun – was a great way of oiling the wheels in life. But, as I was soon to find out, those wheels also had a very nasty habit of falling off.

3

YOU FAT BASTARD

A picture of my 17-year-old-self popped up on my phone the other day. I have to say I look pretty damned good. I was a fit lad. Six-foot-two, strong, great set of legs. People think there were times as a player when I was like an elephant, but if you take a good look at me you'll see I've got big shoulders and a massive head. It must have been a real pleasure for Mum when she gave birth. In fact, so big is my head that when I had my last pair of glasses made, bespoke in Harrogate of course, the optician told me I'd got the biggest head he'd ever seen. He nearly had to go to B&Q to get a bigger tape measure. He was adamant he meant his comment as a compliment – I took a little bit of convincing.

When I look back at that other photo of myself, the one beneath the dartboard, I have to concede that the big head and shoulders excuse wasn't quite washing anymore. But while that image shocks me now, at the time I thought my size wasn't anything to worry about. 'Lose that bit of stomach and you'll be all right,' I'd tell myself. I was Mr Next Week. I'll start dieting – next week. I'll cut down on the booze – next week. I'll start getting out and walking more – next week. If you recognise a bit of Mr Next Week in yourself, I'll tell you now, next week never comes.

To be fair, I had occasionally tried diets – 'No carbs before Marbs' as they say on the *The Only Way Is Essex*, which in English translates to lay off the carbs if you're heading off to Marbella and want to squeeze yourself into a bikini. I wasn't that bothered about a bikini but fitting into a pair of swim shorts would have been nice. Whatever diet I tried, the only certainty was that it wouldn't last long. I was trying to lose weight with fad diets, but then as soon as I started eating normally I'd put it all back on and then some. I've always thought of myself as someone with willpower. Someone who could make himself run through a brick wall if he had to. But when it came to food, it was different. I was addicted. I couldn't stop. It was a constant craving and I had no choice but to give in to it. Food was the only thing that could bring me comfort. Definitely, 100 per cent, addicted. It was another mad, bad, sad or glad thing – whatever the emotion, food was the answer. The weight wasn't slapped on overnight. I'd ballooned steadily, about half a stone a year. As daft as it sounds, my size crept up on me. The problem with that is there comes a day when you catch yourself in the mirror. SHIT! You then start with the big con: 'Well, if I put it on, I can take it off. It can't be that hard.' But actually it's a big ask – in your head it actually seems impossible. And all the time the strain you're putting your health under is getting greater and greater.

The heavier I got, the worse my snoring got. Which wasn't great because it was already registering on the Richter scale. In the end, I went in the spare bedroom because my wife Leah could hardly get any kip. One night her and my two girls, Pebbles and Kizzy, heard me talking in my sleep. They crept closer and put their ears to the door. 'Roast dinner!' I was moaning. 'Roast dinner!' Another time I had a dream about this amazing Chinese. That night, I actually had to go out and get it. We'd laugh, but there was no escaping how twisted and damaging my relationship with food was. There were times when Leah would pretty much beg me not to eat as much. I would have a massive pile of toast and then twenty minutes later be complaining that I was starving. Leah would tell me it was impossible, but my head would be telling me something completely different. I needed that food. I had to have it. If I was away, doing a charity event or an after-dinner, I'd stop at fast food places, have whatever I wanted, no second thoughts. It got to the point where Leah started doing me healthy packed lunches. When I got back, she'd find them dumped on the back seat underneath a pile of McDonald's wrappers. It wasn't just Leah's words I ignored, it was my brothers'. Mum was on my case as well, plus pretty much everyone else in our family as well as close friends. Again and again they'd try to make me see sense about my weight, about the damage I was doing to myself, and again and again I didn't listen. Truthfully, I didn't want to listen. 'I know, I know,' I'd say. But I was just paying lip service. What I really meant was, 'Shut up, I don't want to hear.'

Everyone around me could tell my weight was getting me down, but when you're in that position you don't always realise the cycle of negative thinking you've got yourself into. By that I mean just how much you've stopped liking yourself. When you're feeling down it's like you stop thinking about anything. Life's just something that's happening around you. You're staring at it through a frosted window. I wasn't worried about myself, because I didn't have the mental capacity to do so. It was like I'd been a Duracell bunny and then someone had taken the batteries out. I was powerless to effect anything. The desire to change has got to come from within. And I had absolutely zero desire to do anything.

You can hide away all you want from the damage a bad lifestyle does to you but it'll find you in the end. And that's exactly what happened when in 2019 I headed off to film the second series of *Harry's Heroes*, the ITV show where my old West Ham boss Harry Redknapp brought together a bunch of ex-England players and pitched them against their German counterparts. To be honest, I hadn't been feeling too good during the first series, although I felt a lot better when we beat Germany 4–2, like we always do. Second time round we headed to France for a rematch. By then I was beginning to get worried. I didn't tell anyone, but I was having frequent dizzy spells. At the same time my memory was going all blurry and I'd have no idea where I was. This was happening for minutes at a time and often twice a day. I'd find myself sitting down in a trance. And then I'd flip out of it and be back to normal. I didn't know what it was, but I knew for sure that something was wrong. Things I'd taken for granted just weren't working anymore. Walking just a few yards would make me feel out of breath and totally spaced out. Going to the supermarket, I'd drive Leah mad by squeezing into the tightest space near the door rather than park 50 yards away. She knew exactly what was going on, same as when I'd hum a tune when I walked upstairs at home to hide the puffing and wheezing.

It got to the stage where I'd deliberately not do things if it meant I had to walk. One time I came out of Chester Racecourse and saw a bit of a hill back up to the town. Not that far, 300 yards tops, but I looked at it, turned round and hailed a cab. A similar thing happened when I went on a golf trip to Bognor Regis. The course was at the bottom of a hill, the hotel at the top. Again, not far, just a few hundred yards. I'd only walked a quarter of the way and I've never been happier to see a bench. When I got halfway, a mate took one look at me: 'Right, stay there. I'm going to fetch the car.' Same if I went to visit someone and they lived in a first-floor flat. Walk up? Sod that. Where's the lift? I wouldn't even book a restaurant if I couldn't park outside. You think that's mad? Get this. Playing pairs at golf, with a hundred quid riding on each hole, there were times when I'd rather lose the money than get out of the buggy, walk to the ball and try to sink the putt. My playing partner would be ripping his hair out. 'You used to play top-flight football week in, week out and now you can't be bothered to get out of this buggy to sink a three-foot putt and win a hundred quid?!' His mouth would literally be hanging open, but nothing he could say would ever change my mind. When it came to getting out of that buggy I simply couldn't be arsed. Anyway, I could have fun sat exactly where I was. I liked to see what angle I could drive the buggy at before it tipped over. Again, not so much fun for the person in the passenger seat. But the maddest thing of all? Not going on holiday abroad. Why? Because I couldn't even face the thought of walking the distance to the boarding gate at Gatwick. Disney World in Florida was out of the question because of that. I would actually make my kids go without that once-in-a-lifetime holiday because I couldn't be bothered to walk those few hundred yards. But that was what I was like.

Inside, I began to panic. It felt like everything, body and mind, was giving up. At that point, dementia in footballers was making the headlines. My mate Alan Shearer had just done a programme on it. But as ever I kept all that worry to myself. Didn't tell the missus, the doctor, anyone. If I was getting dementia, I didn't want to know the truth – typical bloke, eh? – but at the same time I knew I was a prime candidate. How many times in your career do you head the ball as a central defender? And that's without all the knocks and collisions. I was forever banging heads with big ugly strikers. The evidence was there for everyone to see. Half the 1966 World Cup winning team had been affected by dementia. Nobby Stiles had it severely before he died in 2020. I'm good friends with Nobby's son John, himself a former midfielder with Leeds United and Doncaster Rovers, who's campaigned tirelessly about the illness, and I couldn't even bring myself to share my worries with him.

Now I was out in France and the dizzy spells were still happening. Not that I let it get in the way of a few beers with my teammates, a drinking session that sparked a bit of drama which I'm pretty sure has been viewed a thousand times more on YouTube than anything I ever did on a football pitch. Next morning at breakfast, Paul Merson had a go at me for my antics in the bar. At least I thought he was having a go at me. Merse was actually massively upset to see me, a mate, someone he'd grown up with and travelled all through the England age groups alongside, not facing up to the fact that was staring me in the face. That if I carried on like I was I'd soon be dead. The reason I had a go back at him and stormed out was simple: I knew he was telling the truth. There was also a bit of me thinking, 'Hang on, you've been addicted to booze, gambling and cocaine, and you're telling me what to do?' But of course that was the whole point. If anyone knows what they're talking about, it's Merse. He was one of the first to come out and speak openly about his demons. When he said he was 'scared, confused, frightened' about what was happening to me, I realised I felt exactly the same. I was in tears when we made up, because I knew he'd done what he'd done from a place of love. If the tables had been turned, I'd have done exactly the same for him.

Fair to say that if I hadn't done *Harry's Heroes* I'd most likely be dead. It was the shock to the system that finally made me realise time was running out. A couple of days later, with the sudden dizzy spells still happening, I left the show and went to have some tests, meeting the lovely German consultant Dr Grosser. It didn't take him long to work out what was wrong. 'Your heart is like that of a 78-year-old man,' he told me.

I don't think he was expecting my reaction, 'Thank God for that!' Remember, I thought I had dementia.

Dr Grosser was quick to point out that having a dicky heart isn't something to celebrate. Truth was, the thing was going haywire. Even when I was resting it was hammering away at 140 beats a minute. I was sitting down and running a marathon at the same time.

It had never occurred to me there was something wrong with my heart. It might have been beating fast, but I just thought that was how blokes my age felt.

'Your blood pressure's so high,' Dr Grosser told me, 'that if someone put a hole in you, you'd be a human fountain.' He was a funny German as well as a lovely one, although not everything he said had me in fits of laughter.

'The way you are now,' he added, 'I'll give you two months.' I looked at the doc. 'Two months to live? What's he on about? He must have got that wrong. I'm Razor, I'm invincible.'

He assured me what he was saying was right. 'What we've got to do,' he told me, 'is turn you back into a normal bloke in his fifties.' Not quite the Bionic Man, but I'd take it.

The good doctor sent me home with a heart monitor to wear during sleep. Its recordings were amazing – my heart was stopping three times a night for eight seconds. It's actually not that unusual for people's hearts to stop for two or three seconds. That's the feeling we get when we suddenly jerk awake. That dream where we're falling off a cliff is actually our bodies waking us up to get everything back to normal. But eight seconds is getting a bit extreme.

Dr Grosser recommended a reset, a bit like when your satellite box is playing up and you turn it off and on at the mains. Basically, the medics kill you – well, how else do you describe it when someone deliberately stops your heart? – and then hopefully get you up and running again at the normal rate. I imagine when most patients hear this, their heart rate increases to about 250 beats a minute. But I wasn't actually scared. I trusted Dr Grosser completely. The 1966 World Cup Final was, after all, a long time ago. And he was completely honest with me from the start. They'd give it seven attempts and if it hadn't worked by then I wouldn't be coming back to life. Everyone would pack up and go home. Except me. Maybe I should have haggled for a couple more goes, but I've never been much good at that kind of thing. I always pay full price for a rug. And anyway, Dr Grosser was great at putting my mind at rest. 'This is the first time I've ever done it,' he explained, 'but I've Googled it and you'll be all right.' As I say, funny guy!

The actual procedure is called cardioversion and involves using a defibrillator to send electric signals to the heart through sticky pads on the chest. It worked for me on the third attempt. Thankfully the recovery period is swift and I was home the same day. So Dr Grosser did come good – 'the lad done well' as they say on *Match of the Day* – and I started to feel better. They killed me to keep me alive, and I was happy with that.

While I was recovering I was grateful to John Hartson, my old West Ham teammate, for getting in touch. I'd messaged John a lot when he'd had his own brush with death, somehow coming through a nightmare time with a brain tumour, and he'd appreciated it. Now the shoe was on the other foot and he was texting me every day. John told me how hard it had hit him when people he thought cared about him hadn't got in touch. Whether that's because people don't know what to say, or are embarrassed, who knows? But he didn't want that to happen to me, and at such a low point in my life I was really thankful for that. As it was, I did receive a load of messages from players. Most of them said the same thing: 'We were worried about you but didn't know what to do.' I'd stopped talking to so many friends; people who I'd helped in the past and wanted to do the same for me in return. But I didn't know how to be the one who needed helping. It had always been the other way round.

As well as the reset, I had a pacemaker fitted to make sure the heartbeat was regulated when I was asleep, with the machine sending data back to the doctors so they could keep an eye on me. A word of warning here – when it comes to asking a mate to take you to the hospital to have a pacemaker put in, pick someone at least half sensible. It was an in and out the same day job and so my pal sat in the car park waiting. A bit bored, he decided to pass the time by sending me endless funny videos. Bear in mind I'm sat on a heart ward with a load of blokes with dodgy tickers – and I'm showing them all these videos. We're all turning purple, gasping for breath, pissing ourselves. In the end, a nurse came in, bollocked me, and actually separated me from the group. Of course, when I rang my pal he found it absolutely hilarious. He'd still have been laughing at the inquest.

I still have to go in for a check-up every six months. The data tells them everything. 'Bloody hell,' they told me one time, 'you had a good Bank Holiday!' Clearly, they could see I'd pushed the boat out a bit, but equally they reassured me that it was OK to go a little bit mad every now and then because my heart would return to normal afterwards.

It was only when I knew I had a future back in the land of the living that I admitted to Leah and the kids how bad I'd been. How close I was to departing for that big changing room in the sky. Another two months and who knows what might have happened. No way in that time would I have gone to the doctor for a check-up myself. I didn't want to know. Simple as that. And I'm not alone. Most blokes are like that. If we've got something wrong with the car, it's making a funny noise or whatnot, we take it to a mechanic and get it fixed. But more than once I've heard blokes say they've got a pain in their chest but don't want to see a doctor in case it's bad news and they can't play golf next week or go away for a bit of sun with the family. Ex-sportspeople are especially bad for it because they've been exposed to an environment where, the minute you admit there's something wrong, the axe falls and you're out of the team. The fact that once I did find out my heart was in trouble, I was happy to get help, while I was scared witless of finding out I had dementia, says a lot also about the underlying fear men have of addressing anything that's wrong up top.

While my heart had been rescued from the brink, there still remained the little – well, big – matter of the weight. I was feeling increasingly ashamed of my size. Every time I stepped into the dreaded specialist 'big men's' clothes shop I'd catch my reflection in the mirror and wonder, 'What the hell has happened to me?' Shopping for clothes was always the worst embarrassment. I'd go into all the usual stores, wander round for a few minutes, and just give up. I'd joke that the only thing I could find that fitted me was aftershave. Always laughing, you see. Always best to make a joke of it. But truth was, it was a total humiliation not to find anything

I could get into. I mean, these places cater for the masses – big, small, and everyone in between. We're not talking some PVC boutique on the King's Road. These shops are where everyday people go to get clothes – except when it came to this everyday person none of them fitted. Even stuff I ordered online would come up too small. It began to affect areas of my life that actually gave me a bit of an escape from the mental misery. The golf bag gathered dust in a corner because none of my stuff fitted me. As I grew, my wardrobe shrank. All I had were the same few old hoodies and joggers to put on over and over again. I wouldn't go to the beach with the kids and have a laugh, wouldn't go to the park, wouldn't walk the dogs. All because I was so embarrassed. But those things were exactly what I needed to get myself out of this deep, deep rut.

It reached the point where I didn't want to leave the house at all. Which meant when the Covid lockdown came along, coinciding with my recovery from the heart op, it was a relief. I didn't want to go out and now I had the perfect excuse not to. The pressure to meet people, to go places, was lifted. Instead, I just started eating and eating. Apps like Deliveroo and Just Eat meant I could sit there and order what I liked when I liked from my phone. I was even ordering ice cream from the local Co-op. And I'd order loads, getting lazier and lazier. At the same time I'd be knocking back cans of cider. I got myself into such a bad routine. At my heaviest during Covid, I was 27 stone. Crazy. Huge. Twice the size I was as a player. I hated myself for what I'd become. You're already feeling down in the dumps and now on top of that you're stuck there as someone you can't stand the sight of. I knew I had to do something about it, but when your confidence and self-esteem are on the floor it's easier said than done. The gym was the obvious place to start, but I couldn't bear the thought of going on my own. If there's a few of you doing the same workout, like in a team, fair enough. But on my own? No way.

It's a vicious circle. You feel terrible so you eat and drink more. The shame you feel from doing that makes you feel worse. And so on and so on. It's like you're driving down a one-way street and every hundred yards someone shuts off the road behind you. Ahead of you is one thing – oblivion.

What finally bulldozed that mental barrier away was a chance meeting with *The Only Way Is Essex* star James Argent at a charity football match in south London. I couldn't believe what I was seeing. Last time I'd seen any pictures of him he looked massive, like me. And now here he was in front of me looking absolutely amazing. It was like he'd lost 10 stone.

I was straight in there: 'How've you done that?' Arge told me he'd actually lost 13 stone. He also told me how. He'd had an operation to fit a gastric sleeve and 70 per cent of his stomach had been removed. That was all I needed to hear. Literally just a two-minute chat. I couldn't take my eyes off the bloke as he walked off. 'Why can't I be like that? I wonder if I could . . .' I had to get home and tell Leah. She wasted no time getting in touch with the clinic and setting the ball rolling. I knew the sleeve was my only chance and I wasn't going to waste it.

Of course, you don't just rock up, knock on the door and have three-quarters of your stomach removed. As a big bloke, you're naturally going to have ongoing health issues. With me the biggest issue they discovered was sleep apnoea, where your breathing stops and starts while you sleep. It meant, without realising it, I was waking up dozens of times a night. Not only does that make you feel knackered a lot of the time, but it can also lead to high blood pressure, heart disease and a higher chance of having a stroke. Sorting it out meant wearing an oxygen mask in bed, like something a fighter pilot would use, although at no point did Leah mistake me for Tom Cruise in *Top Gun*. I also had to go on a strict diet for six months before the op. Unlike other times I'd gone on diets, because I bought into the sleeve and everything it offered me – not least of which was a new chance at life – I never fell off the wagon.

Finally, six months after the initial enquiry, I had the operation. Basically, they put a big elastic band halfway up my stomach. In one go, that took 70 per cent of it away. From then on, that's it. When that other 30 per cent is full up, you can't get hungry anymore. The sleeve also acts as an appetite suppressant, affecting the hormone that makes you want food.

I was in and out of the hospital in twenty-four hours, no pain at all. I kept waiting and it never came, like nothing had ever happened. I was half expecting one of the doctors to tell me they hadn't gone through with it, but soon enough it was pretty obvious they had. The result was amazing. The weight dropped off from the start. By the time I 'came out' about the op by putting a picture up on Twitter a few months later, I was 7 stone lighter without me even trying. All I could think was, 'I wish I'd had it done years ago.' I'll be honest, you do hear the odd horror story about gastric sleeves – that people who've had them are sick all the time, things like that. I'm so, so lucky to be able to eat what I want. I've only been sick once since I had the gastric sleeve and that was off Leah's homemade spaghetti bolognese. Nothing to do with her, she's a great cook – it was just too rich.

I was so happy. And then people started commenting, the usual dickheads popping up, accusing me of 'cheating', although naturally no-one actually said anything to my face. It was so stupid that it was laughable. First up, weight loss isn't a game. Second up, the only thing I was cheating was death. Without an immediate weight reduction, I was staring into an early grave. No two ways about it, that operation saved my life, and thankfully the vast majority of replies to my post recognised what a big deal it was for me. In all, that Twitter post received 10 million views. Having spent so long with my confidence, my self-esteem, totally gone, one thought dominated my thinking: 'I'm back. People love me again.' Losing weight straightaway made me so happy. I could do simple things, like comply with Leah's rule that if I needed a number two, I had to use the upstairs toilet! That's fifteen stairs. Before the op, I'd struggle every time. Now I was positively bounding up there, Andrex in hand. Not the nicest anecdote you'll ever read – apologies if you're having your lunch – but it says a lot about where I was at physically, pre-op. I also run up there to fetch my glasses whereas beforehand I'd be watching TV with my face screwed up because I couldn't be arsed. Even getting the remote from the other side of the room was too much trouble. I'd ask one of the kids to do it for me. And remember, this is a bloke whose job it was to run and run. Best of all, we've got a trampoline in the garden and no longer does it collapse when I look at it.

There was another thing. After so long feeling self-conscious, I felt comfortable going out. Don't get me wrong, specialist big men's shops do a great service, but I just felt so ashamed. I threw those clothes away as quick as I could. When I did a spread for the one of the papers about my weight loss, and the photographer wanted me in that classic pose – in a pair of massive trousers, holding the waistband out at the front – it felt good to tell him, 'Forget it, mate, they've gone.'

In every way imaginable, the gastric sleeve has been a massive step forward towards a better life. Talking of steps, the weight loss means my knees don't hurt anymore. Up to now I've lost 11 stone. I couldn't put that weight back on even if I wanted to. No chance of seeing the relapse photo of me as I wheel my shopping trolley full of pizzas and pies out of the supermarket. My relationship with food has totally changed. The kitchen has gone from my downfall to my safe space.

You might recall I made the final of *MasterChef* in 2019 and I prepare some pretty amazing stuff, even if I say so myself, mainly vegetarian, although I do cook the occasional white meat, chicken or turkey dish. Leah knows how much cooking means to me and is forever buying me new gadgets – crockpots, air fryers, and the like. It's the mess I make she doesn't like. 'Look,' I tell her, 'it's the price for me still being alive!'

Don't get me wrong, if I go out for a curry I'll still order three dishes. The difference is, I'll just have a mouthful of each one, no rice. I might only eat a fiver's worth but I still get sixty quid's worth of satisfaction. Compare that to the Razor of old. The worst version of me could have eighteen pints and four curries. Thousands upon thousands of calories – bad calories – in just a few hours. That's the beauty of having the sleeve. I can eat anything I want – cakes, curries, the lot – but only a little bit. At home I eat out of a kid's bowl. I'm full up now after a quarter of a jacket potato. After four mouthfuls I literally feel like I've had a roast dinner. Today for breakfast I had a little Rice Krispies bar and I was full to the brim. It's given me an even better idea for my next book – *The Gastric Sleeve Chef: A Small Portion of Razor Ruddock*. Let's face it, if you can only have four mouthfuls, it's got to be good food. The only downside of the sleeve is I can't eat and drink at the same time. There has to be half an hour between or else I'll be sick. I also don't get hunger pains, I just start burping. Apologies if you're sitting next to me on the train.

But I'll apologise for nothing else. I'm proud of myself for making that reset. If I hadn't got a gastric sleeve, I wouldn't be here now. Everyone around me says the same: that I've cheated the Grim Reaper. Duncan Ferguson was nothing compared to him. And looking back, I have to agree. I'd been on a collision course with serious ill-health for a long, long time.

4

OLD SPICE

Drink used to rule my life. Win and I'd drink to celebrate. Lose and I'd drink to change how I felt. Draw and I'd get pissed anyway.

The key words are 'used to'. These days it's a couple of glasses of wine rather than fifteen pints. I can actually quite happily go for a meal without drinking at all. I've become a connoisseur of tap water. But reaching that stage has been a bit of a journey. All right, a hell of a journey. I've probably thrown an Olympic-sized swimming pool of beer, wine and spirits down my neck over the years. No wonder in the end I found myself drowning in the deep end.

I wasn't alone. Dressing rooms were different then. The phrase 'alpha male' wasn't really used in the nineties, but in a football dressing room the lead alpha was the biggest drinker and the biggest shagger. They were the heroes. If it happened to be the same person then they took on superhero status. I was never going to win the best shagger trophy, but when it came to drinking I definitely made the play-offs a few times.

Alcohol was the order of the day wherever I played. The pub was the natural environment for bonding with your fellow players. At Southampton I spent some great times with seasoned pros like Jimmy Case, Russell Osman and Glenn Cockerill. I always joke that Jimmy taught me two great skills – how to hurt people and how to drink. I tried my best, but truth is, I could never match him in either. Jimmy could also drink and be quiet, something else I never quite mastered. My default position right from the point I started drinking was to do so in as loud a way as possible. Having two big brothers just made me worse. From day one in our house I was fighting to be heard. By the time I was standing at bars, I was very highly skilled. Me and my brothers are still loud. We can't go out together too often as it's just too much, probably for us and definitely for anyone unfortunate enough to be nearby. Once every three months, that's enough.

At every club, I was blessed with people who I could be very loud around. My first day at Liverpool I met Jamie Redknapp and Steve McManaman at a hotel in town and straightaway they took me to a karaoke bar down the docks for a few 'scoops' – the first time I'd ever heard that particular way of describing a few beers. It was only a matter of time before I was up there singing my old favourite 'Strangers In The Night'. I've always loved a bit of karaoke. I'd have a go at bringing out a record like Chris Kamara, but I can't shake off the memory of finishing second in *Stars In Their Eyes* – behind one of the Dingles off *Emmerdale*. I'm pretty sure that's not going to secure me an album deal or the legends' spot at Glastonbury. Anyway, I had a great time at the karaoke bar and because we played for Liverpool, we weren't charged for any of it. Same thing happened when we went for a Chinese in town. I was reaching for my wallet when the lads stopped me. 'No, Razor, when you play for Liverpool, you don't pay for anything.'

I went to bed happier than ever that I'd made the right move, rising the next day for another tough engagement – a golf day at Royal Birkdale in nearby Southport, one of the finest courses in the country. Again, the drink flowed. After the round, we all got absolutely smashed. For once it wasn't me making the headlines. That particular distinction fell to Don Hutchison, who at one point emerged from a pub toilet with a Budweiser label over his privates. This wouldn't have mattered so much had not someone, presumably with a strong zoom lens, taken a few snaps and sold them to the

papers. As introductions to a new club go, a piss-up in a karaoke bar and a bloke appearing in public with his tackle behind
a beer label was a promising start. 'What a football club!' I
thought. 'WHAT A FOOTBALL CLUB!'

I went to Liverpool at a time of change. There was the old
guard – players like John Barnes, Ronnie Whelan, Jan Molby,
Bruce Grobbelaar – who'd seen it, done it and got about
twenty-five T-shirts, and the new guard, the likes of Macca
and Jamie, Robbie Fowler, David James and Jason McAteer.
With the Spice Girls topping the charts at the time, the
media, being imaginative types, soon dubbed this new crop
of players 'the Spice Boys'. I tried to get in that little circle
of well-preened, smooth-skinned, hair-gelled youngsters but
only qualified as Old Spice. I've still got a bottle of the stuff at
home by way of a tribute.

Interestingly, 30 miles down the road the media narra-
tive around Manchester United was totally different. There
were just as many young party boys at Old Trafford but they
weren't called the Spice Boys, they were 'Fergie's Fledglings',
presumably waiting patiently in their nest for Alex Ferguson
to bring them a dead vole. Fergie's Fledglings were an apparently great bunch of lads who were only interested in lacing
their boots up and getting out there and bringing glory to

United. It was like the 1930s and they were in black and white on some old cigarette cards. The fact they were living exactly the same life as us, having a drink, in and out of nightclubs, never seemed to move the dial on how they were perceived. Arsenal was the same. They had a batch of young players who also very much liked to enjoy themselves, but that was seen as unifying, as team-building. Liverpool's youngsters, on the other hand, were, if you believed what you read in some of the papers, a bunch of full-of-themselves lads who preferred chasing fun and fame over working hard on the football pitch. The somewhat less sensational reality was that the younger players had bought new apartments down at the docks – which last time I checked wasn't a crime – and as single lads would be seen every now and again in the bars around town. It was hardly 'Hold the front page!' material.

With me being married with kids, the younger lads loved nothing more than winding me up about being able to go out where they wanted when they wanted. But I wasn't bothered. My local in Formby was fantastic, so good in fact that they'd travel out from Liverpool and stay over at my place. I had a seven-bedroom house, classic footballer's gaff, with a converted garage out the back where we'd stay up and watch all the big fights – Mike Tyson at four in the morning, all that kind of stuff. I had a giant telly, big speakers, glass-fronted fridges full of beer, the lot. It was a proper party house.

We liked each others' company and found excuses to spend more time together, a racehorse being one of them. Some Horse we called it, Robbie Fowler's suggestion after the racing authorities had turned down Betty Swollocks. He liked the idea of the course commentator having to say, 'and coming up on the right-hand side, Some Horse' or 'Some Horse has unseated its rider at the first bend.' Some Horse wasn't ever expected to set the horseracing world on fire – it had about as much chance of being put out to stud as Jason McAteer – but did pull off a shock when it won at 55–1 at Pontefract on the Tote. We were jumping up and down, hugging each other, cheering, celebrating, when we realised we'd have doubled our money had we bothered walking 50 yards further and put our cash on with a bookie who had it at 100–1.

Having a racehorse was another good social ruse. We could say it was running anywhere and use it as an excuse to get away for a few drinks. It was only a nag and so the chances of anyone finding out it was actually spending the day asleep in a stable were minimal. I was just about to pretend Some Horse was running in the Ibizan Grand National when the trainer told us it was injured and advised us to give it away.

Which, being a bunch of footballers who couldn't be arsed with the effort of doing anything else, we did. I sometimes wonder what became of Some Horse. Maybe it made a comeback under a different name. For all us lot knew, it could have won the Derby.

Ignorant about off-track matters I might have been, but unlike my fellow owners I did actually have a short-lived career in the saddle, climbing aboard to race against a select bunch of retired footballers at Kempton Park. My horse was ex-police, so there was immediate friction, but representing Liverpool I came third behind Kerry Dixon (Chelsea) and the winner Steve Lomas (Manchester City). To be fair to my mount, it was carrying a little more weight than the others.

Other times, like any group of pals, we might go away together; a time to forget the pressures of football and also revel in the acute daftness of McAteer. When a few of us went on holiday to Ibiza and rented a minibus for the thirty-minute ride to the coast, Jason climbed onboard with a massive bag of ice.

'Jase, what are you doing?'

'It's ice, to keep the beers cool on the beach.'

'But it's thirty-five degrees. It'll melt before we even get there.'

'Oh yeah,' he considered. 'I'll go and fetch a spare.'

Jason was known as Dave in our dressing room, the name that the spectacularly dozy Trigger from *Only Fools and Horses* always called Rodney. We'd have called him Trigger but that name had already gone to Rob Jones, a man who once asked how he'd recognise the bride at a wedding. It was a shame because Jason had been called Trigger at his previous club, Bolton Wanderers, and really did deserve the name. I'll never forget being with him when he locked his car keys in his new Porsche outside his house. Taking pity on him, a passing police officer offered to try to open it up using the old trick of sliding a coat hanger down the gap between the window and the handle. 'If you could just fetch me a hanger, sir?' Thirty seconds later Jason appeared with a wooden one. Based on an application Jason made for a credit card I'm not quite sure how he was ever allowed near enough money to buy a sports car. Filling in the form he turned to me: 'Raze, it says here "position in company". What shall I put? Right-back or midfield?' Thankfully, Jason was a much better footballer than he was *Brain of Britain* contender.

The older lads at Liverpool weren't part of the younger boys' activities not because they disapproved, more because they'd been there and done it. They'd travelled the world, won everything, been to every pub and nightclub in Liverpool ten times over. While they went home after a few beers, the younger single lads would party on. I got a glimpse early on of how the older players lived when the legend that was Ronnie Whelan invited me over to his house to play snooker. He had a trophy cabinet nearly as big as all my drinks fridges put together, medals and mementos for everything – European Cups, FA Cups, League Cups, the lot.

Out of all the Spice Boys I was probably closest to Jamie Redknapp, who I roomed with all the way through my time with Liverpool. It made sense. Me and Jamie had been kids together at Tottenham, which is how I also knew his dad Harry before I went to West Ham. I remember actually saying to Jamie at that time, when things at Liverpool had hit a low, 'Please, mate, do me a favour, get Harry to sign me!' Jamie was a good-looking lad – still is in a dark room – and so would have girls falling over themselves to be near him. How delighted he must have been then to spend so many nights with me, a commitment I repaid by trying to get him fined as often as humanly possible. In football, there's so many fines that it's pretty much impossible to avoid them. My own personal favourite was when mobile phones arrived and players would be penalised if theirs rang during a team meeting. I'd sit there and secretly ring Jamie's. The manager would be straight on it: 'Right, Jamie! Five hundred quid!' Jamie really should have learned that lesson faster. The way I saw it, the more fines we had, the better booze-up we'd have at the end of the season, because the fines provided the kitty. Jamie did more than most to give the rest of the lads a great day out. Actually, those early mobiles were a constant source of joy. If anyone left theirs unattended for a moment, the language would be immediately switched to Russian. And the instructions on how to turn it back to English would be in Russian too.

To be fair to Jamie, he did get his own back when I was invited on to *A League of Their Own*, the Sky show where he's a weekly panellist. I was wheeled on naked, face down on a trolley, in a competition to see which team could best sponge me down. You'd be right in thinking sports quiz shows have moved on a bit from the days of Billy Beaumont and Emlyn Hughes on *A Question of Sport*. What happened next on this occasion was Jamie's hand somehow ended up somewhere it shouldn't have been. I've never been shy, and my nude appearances on *A League of Their Own* have become a feature down the years, possibly the most infamous being as a police stripogram, when I ripped off my helmet (no, not that one), shirt, jacket and thong in front of the two Jamies, Redknapp and Carragher, who were actually expecting something a little more pleasing on the eye until yours truly appeared. For me the highlight of a cultured routine was the finale when I wiped my privates on Jamie Carragher's face and my arse on the back of Jamie Redknapp's head. I remain available for bookings if anyone's interested. Another time I appeared as a life model, lying in elegant pose on a chaise longue. I think more than anything it was the size of my balls that shocked the assembled celebrity artists. I always prided myself on having the biggest Niagras in the football league. Boxers have regularly asked me if they can use them as a punchbag.

I've never cared what the media thought about me, but the Spice Boys tag caused a problem in that once elements of the press had delivered their chosen label, the whole team was forever judged against it. So when the so-called Spice Boys then turned up at Wembley for the 1996 FA Cup Final in those bloody awful cream-coloured Emporio Armani suits, plus white Gucci shoes, it just made the whole thing a million times worse. The minute that image was seen around the world it ensured one thing and one thing only – if Liverpool lost the game, the whole thing would be blamed on a few players putting fashion above football. People – fans and the media especially – are fickle. If we'd won, they'd have been the best suits the world had ever seen (the shoes would still have been a bit shit) and attention would have turned to the stuff those Man United boys were doing off the pitch. But that wasn't the way it panned out and instead those infamous threads became a coal sack those players would drag around forever.

The suits were seen as a symptom of the problem. They represented a side to that Liverpool team which some parts of the media had decided they didn't like. But when judging how people were back in the mid-nineties and early 2000s, it's easy to forget just how laddish the culture was back then, with magazines like *Loaded* and *Maxim* flying off the shelves and *Soccer AM* parading a 'Soccerette', a female football fan, up and down a catwalk every Saturday morning. Those magazines, plus the tabloids, wanted footballers to be part of the 'lad' scene. They wanted photos of Stevie Mac, of Jamie, of Robbie, David Beckham (surely the only true Spice Boy footballer, having married one of them) on the front cover. They wanted stories of players out on the piss. They wanted big, in-your-face, geezerish interviews. Footballers were becoming the new A-listers – music, fashion, football, all interlinked. David James was actually the face of Armani, possibly the biggest designer brand of the lot. And so if a team was going to walk out at Wembley in beige Armani suits, 1996 was 100 per cent the time it was going to happen, the exact point when all these worlds collided. In the nineties, we found ourselves live on TV every week. The big broadcast money was coming in. We were part of an exciting new Premier League, or Premiership as it was known back then. Football was changing and footballers were changing with it. Players didn't want to hang out with pop and rock stars anymore. It was the other way round. Robbie Williams wanted to come out with us. It was *him* sat on *our* coach. At Aston Villa, he actually came on our stage – the pitch. It wasn't us being invited to watch a gig of his from the wings. To be fair to Rob, I should mention that no-one was more embarrassed than him to be out on the turf at Villa Park. If it had been Vale Park, it might have been a bit different.

I see 'Spice Boys' now as the group equivalent of 'Razor' – a name that followed a group of players around that they couldn't shake off. The truth was those players, like me, never gave anything other than their total best for Liverpool. Their commitment to the cause was unshakeable – remember, Jason and Robbie had grown up as Liverpool fans, while Macca, although Everton as a kid, had been with the club since the age of 14. Roy Evans once said that if he could, he'd have eleven Robbie Fowlers in his team because that way he'd never lose. Just because you like a night out every now and again doesn't make you a bad person or a bad player. Neither does it mean you're arrogant. Selfish characters don't survive at football clubs. They're divisive and destroy team spirit. The team is everything and if a player doesn't buy into that then no-one wants them around, just the same as if a player isn't giving their all then the coaches and manager will soon kick their arse down the road.

There are always 'what ifs' in sport – every pundit out there would be out of a job if there weren't – but to say that Liverpool would have been the team of the nineties had it not been for a few players going out having fun every now and again is ridiculous. There are a thousand reasons why one team wins the league and another finishes third; why one team parades the FA Cup round Wembley while the other sits in the dressing room and licks its wounds. The fact that Robbie Fowler, me, Macca, or anyone else had a few beers and stayed up past midnight every now and again isn't one of them.

In fact, if I had to identify the overriding reason for Liverpool's decline as title contenders in the nineties, I'd pinpoint an arrogance from the club, not the players. Liverpool had been the team of the seventies and eighties, and so there was an attitude of 'why should we start changing the way we do things now?' Nutrition and physiotherapy were nowhere.

Training was all too often just five-a-side for an hour, next goal wins, the kind of stuff you'd find happening on the pitches at the back of a leisure centre. The opposition was never spoken about. Tactics were pretty much non-existent. Play 4–4–2 and give the ball to Barnes and McManaman, that was it. Maybe that 'we do it the Liverpool way, fuck 'em' attitude was OK in the past when teams were pretty much the same in what they were doing off the pitch – i.e. nothing – but times had changed. Clubs were becoming increasingly technical in how they trained, a new era of footballer athletes was coming in.

At Liverpool, on the other hand, the only real consideration was how much you weighed. That meant quick fixes rather than long-term plans. Dehydration in particular ruled the day. Before the scales came out, you'd go to the kitchen, get a black sack, put your kit on over the top of it and run around for a bit. You weren't losing weight, you were just getting more and more dehydrated, maybe dangerously so. The alternative was to get pissed the night before so you'd arrive at training already dehydrated from the alcohol. Once you'd been weighed, you'd drink 6 pints of water to get yourself back to where you should be. Do that over a long enough period, justifying it in your head, and it becomes a habit. Maybe now they'd call it a disorder. But for a long time there was no-one at that club who had the education to say that was a stupid way of doing things, a bad way to treat your body. In the end, I worked out what was good for me myself. At Liverpool I generally weighed between 14 st 10 lb and 15 st. If I was 15 st 1 lb, I'd feel slow and heavy, whereas if I was 14 st 11 lb, I'd feel good and quick. The difference was 4 lb, so physically it wasn't that big a difference, but in my head it was massive. One way or another, I'd try to make sure I was 14 st 11 lb when Saturday at 3 p.m. came round.

Again, this was something I worked out for myself, because the club's way of working out an ideal weight, standing in front of someone with a chart in their hand, wasn't fit for purpose.

'How tall are you, Ruddock?'

'Six-foot-three.'

'Right, six-foot-three. It says here you should be thirteen-and-a-half stone, like your mate over there.' I'd look round at some beanpole.

'Yes, but hang on, I'm a completely different build to him. Can't you see?'

Next, the instrument would come out – that bulldog clip thing where they grab a bit of your waist and pinch it. 'You're 10 per cent bigger than last month, Ruddock.'

'Really? That's quite a lot don't you think? Are you sure you just haven't pinched more?'

It really was a load of bollocks.

Compare that to what was happening at Arsenal, one of the clubs that had taken root in Liverpool's previous home at the top of the table. Ray Parlour would tell me about the nutritional aspects of elite sport that were being instilled in players, right down to chewing every mouthful twenty times to allow the body to extract the maximum value. That's not to say I thought what Arsenal were doing was necessarily the way forward. If anything, it sounded nuts. Dieticians? Can't eat what you want? What's all that about? I'd grown up around players like Matt Le Tissier whose regular pre-match intake was a trip to McDonald's. But then again, if Ray Parlour, a bloke who liked living life to the full, was up for it, then who was I to say it wasn't a good idea?

Forget long runs, endless five-a-sides, Ray also told me how training at Arsenal was for short eight-minute bursts. Again, I was astonished. Eight minutes? How could that work? It flew in the face of everything football had been to that point. Thing is, while most clubs, Liverpool included, still had players running round the pitch for half an hour before training even started, Arsene Wenger had been working in a totally different environment out in Monaco. He understood that making players plod around a field doesn't in any way replicate what they're going to experience on the pitch. The game's about short bursts of energy, quick reactions. Go, Stop, Recovery. That's what coaching sessions are now, and that's exactly how they should be.

Wenger had studied the science of the human body. He'd seen what dieticians and doctors could do for performance. Our doctor used to come in on Thursday. If you were injured on Friday, that was the end of it. It might be six days before you'd be seen. There was no-one else to go to. Even when the doctor did turn up, the situation was often farcical. One time, I needed an ultrasound on my knee but there was no gel. Ronnie Moran disappeared into the kitchen and got some washing-up liquid. The club that had spent £2.5 million on me was now squirting my knee with Fairy.

Having no physio worked well on the injuries front – because there was no-one to find anything wrong. Back then, pretty much any footballer with a niggle would go out and play, and it's surprising how often the pain goes away. But that was more luck than science. Truth was that Liverpool, one of the biggest clubs in the world, was being run on an almost amateur basis. It wasn't just the lack of a physio, the club also had no dietician or fitness coach.

Anfield was old school, run by tradition, while 200 miles away at Highbury, Wenger was bulldozing aside that tradition and making massive inroads into the culture around football, the way players lived their lives. To him, everything a player did, mind and body, fed into performance. While doctors and physios were tending to injuries at Arsenal, and, crucially, trying to ensure they didn't happen in the first place, at Liverpool we were rooting around for bags of peas in the freezer. Arsenal was the very latest in detailed medical knowhow. Liverpool was Findus.

This is how far behind Liverpool were – we even had physios at Millwall. And that was when I started there in 1984. A decade later and still Liverpool hadn't caught up. By then the rest of the field were out of sight. When a physio did arrive in the form of Mark Leather, a lovely bloke, known to all and sundry as Judas after he'd gone from Preston to Burnley, or possibly the other way round, before arriving on Merseyside, and who did incredibly well to put things right as quickly as he did, finally we began playing catch-up. But it was like lining up at the Grand National a lap back from everyone else.

When I went to West Ham, I saw another club which had leapt ahead of Liverpool in doing things a different, better, way. OK, Harry Redknapp might have been old-school, but then again he'd only train us for half an hour at the end of the session. Before that we'd have a coach for the warm-up, backed up with fitness coaches and specialist sprint coaches. Foodwise, whereas at Liverpool I'd try to eat healthy, salads and stuff, but know I could always get my hands on a bacon sandwich, at West Ham bread had been replaced by wraps. It was nutrition all the way, a plan we were expected to follow. At Liverpool, you could have gone home and had ice cream and pizza five days a week and no-one would have batted an eyelid. I'll admit sometimes I would take the piss. When one day the physio stuck me on a running machine for forty minutes, then went off to do an X-ray, the minute he disappeared I nipped off for a coffee and a bacon sarnie. I then came back, chucked a load of water over myself and 'collapsed' on the floor. When the physio found me like that he was delighted. Stupid, but it made me laugh that I could be at a club like Liverpool and get away with it. If I'd been part of a concerted club-wide nutrition plan maybe I'd have looked at it in a different way. As it was, off my own back I would go to a sauna on the way to training to help me lose weight at every club I was at. That's me – there was no-one telling me to do it.

All things considered, I'm pretty proud of the fact that in the five full seasons I was at Anfield, we finished in the top four on four occasions, which, while still below Liverpool's seventies and eighties standard, wasn't a bad achievement considering the strides other clubs were taking off the pitch and how significantly they were strengthening on it. Nowadays, with the expansion of the Champions League, to finish in the top four is seen as success in itself. Maybe there wouldn't have been so much nonsense spoken about the Spice Boys if that had been the case in the mid-nineties. They'd have been viewed as footballers doing well, rather than playboys underachieving.

I might not have been an official Spice Boy. I never had an immaculate Louis Vuitton bag full of hair 'product', moisturiser and balm. I never went for pedicures so I'd look good on holiday in my flip-flops. But I didn't look too out of place alongside those chaps on a night out. I was an advert for the old-school. Soap and water never did anyone any harm. Look at me now, skin like a baby's bottom. Well, a baby walrus maybe.

Anyway, like I say, football's fickle. Me? I was never that into the Spice Girls. I preferred Tom Jones.

5

THE FITTER YOU ARE, THE MORE YOU CAN DRINK

One area Liverpool certainly did excel at was drinking. Their Tuesday Club was something of awe.

Tuesday Clubs existed as it was the perfect night, and usually day as well, to have a few drinks because you had the Wednesday off training. People talk about individual clubs having a drinking culture, and Arsenal's Tuesday Club in the eighties and early nineties was infamous, but truth is every club was at it. The only question was to what extent.

At Liverpool, the Tuesday Club would start early doors and end sometime in the early hours of Wednesday morning at The Continental nightclub in town. With there being so many times players couldn't drink, it was hardly surprising that when the opportunity came, they really wanted to go for it. The attitude was simple: 'Right, lads, we've got to get a week's drinking in here!' Clubs turned a blind eye because they were happy for you to go out on a Tuesday and get it out of your system. The other positive for the club was you were out as group rather than in the dribs and drabs that could make you a bit more vulnerable to attention from dickheads. You were also more likely to behave with the senior players around to keep you in check. And Liverpool weren't daft. A big club like that would have its spies out, making sure you were all right, that there was nothing that could turn into trouble. Not that I ever felt that vibe in Liverpool. And anyway, by the time I got there my radar for a bad 'un was quite well tuned. As a footballer, as soon as you have a bit of money there's suddenly shedloads of people who want to know you. Early on it was difficult to know who to trust. After a couple of years as a pro it would take me thirty seconds max to work out whether someone was a nice person or not, an ability I've never lost.

After recovering on Wednesday, on Thursday and Friday we weren't allowed out. At all, for anything. If you were seen picking the kids up from school or out shopping – and somewhere like Liverpool you were bound to be spotted – you'd be fined. Those two days were: 'Train, go home, rest. Train, go home, rest.' And that was it. Even golf was banned forty-eight hours before a game. It was very strict in that way. During my time at Liverpool, a newspaper contacted the club claiming I'd been seen pissed-up in a pub on the lunchtime before a night game. It was ridiculous, not least because we'd stay in a hotel all day before an evening fixture. Even so, they contacted Roy Evans, threatening to print the story. 'Go on then!' he said. 'Do it!' What the newspaper didn't know was that on that particular occasion I'd picked up Roy on the way to the hotel. Myths and legends follow players around, like the coin game story, a bit of nonsense I made up about the Liverpool lads passing a pound coin round during a game, with the one who had it in their hand at the final whistle having to pay for the drinks that night. I said it for a laugh but get asked about it all the time.

While I may occasionally have been wronged, there were plenty of other times when my behaviour was out of order. I wasn't alone. It wasn't uncommon for a few of us to sneak out on Wednesday to The Paradox club in Aintree. Hopefully, that wouldn't get out of hand, but players had ways of getting out of doing too much graft on the training pitch next day if they'd got a bad hangover. Often they'd pull up clutching the back of their leg, claiming an injury. No-one can see inside your leg. If you say it's injured, the coaching staff have to go with it. But coaches aren't stupid. They have their own little ways to work out if you've been on the piss. Liverpool youngster Mark Kennedy used to say to me, 'Don't take your jacket off, Razor, that's how they know.' What he meant was, dehydration the morning after a drink-up meant you'd over-heat quickly. Removing your jacket on a cold day was a dead giveaway you'd been up to no good. Instead, you'd have to keep it on and boil.

If the boss thought the team's socialising was getting out of hand, we'd do our best to convince him that he was worrying unduly. More than once when Roy Evans asked us what we were doing after training, we told him, with great innocence, 'There's a crown green bowls place down the road, gaffer. We're going down there for a few ends.' We never mentioned the pub stuck on the front. Or the fact that it didn't shut halfway through the day if you played for Liver-pool. Occasionally, Roy himself would have a drink with us. Not the Tuesday Club – there has to be a line! But if we were playing abroad and stuck in a hotel pre-season, he'd come out. For the coaching staff it was a chance to relax – and keep an eye on us. If we were in Europe during the regular season, however, rarely would we ever venture from the hotel. The randomness of a cup draw means you can find yourself in places that might be a little bit dodgy. Even somewhere like Rome it can be a bad idea to leave the hotel. You don't know who's about, who might want to have a go at you.

Whatever club I was at, it soon became clear I was one of those people that if you went out with them you could pretty much guarantee something stupid or funny was going to happen. A night out for me was an adventure. I'd have it all planned out: 'Right, we'll meet here, go there, then there, down to there for an hour, and finish off in there.' In my head, a night out was five consecutive games, and each one could have a different result. It was like being a kid again – an hour of Monopoly, an hour of Cluedo and so on. Except board games didn't end with a kebab. Since I was the one taking everyone on the adventure, it was only natural that I'd have to come up with the plan. I was the social secretary at every football club I ever played for, right back to organising the Christmas party for the Millwall lads when I was only 18. Everyone agreed it was the best Christmas party they'd ever had. Strippers, everything. 'Not shy in coming forward!' – that's what people used to say about me. But I used to find organising stuff exciting. I liked the thought of what madness a night could bring.

The best Christmas party of all was at West Ham, a seventies-themed do in beautiful Romford. I'd stayed behind with Trevor Sinclair to settle up in one establishment when the police marched in, investigating an accusation that a bottle had been thrown and a car damaged. Apparently the two people responsible, one black, one white, had been wearing seventies clothing. We were in seventies clothing, one was black and one was white, and so the Old Bill were convinced they had the culprits. Even when I pointed out there were another thirty-eight people out there in seventies clothing, some black, some white, they were convinced it was us, and so off down the nick we went. As they were booking us in, Trevor was sick all over the sergeant's desk. It was Black Eye Friday and there were more than a few locals who'd been nicked that night as well. Trevor's little performance was the best thing they'd seen all night. 'Go on, Trevor! Go on, my son!' With the vomit mopped up, the sergeant asked me to empty my pockets. I promptly plonked four grand on the desk. His eyes nearly popped out of his skull. Maybe he'd pulled in the head of the Essex underworld. 'The kitty,' I explained. 'For our works do.'

To be fair, for someone whose reputation for respecting authority isn't great, I didn't have too many incidents with the boys in blue. As a pro, the only other time was at Tottenham. I was warming up with Teddy Sheringham when I rocketed a ball and accidentally hit a policeman. At first I just thought it had knocked his helmet off – which of course would have been amusing for all concerned – but then, horribly, I found out the ball had hit him in the face and his glasses had smashed in his eyes. He was forced to retire. I felt terrible and made sure to go to his medical tribunal to apologise.

My reputation as a high-class social organiser means that if I've heard 'Where are we going, Razor?' once, I've heard it a million times. Similarly, when I was with my non-football friends, I was always the one who had to go up to the doorman: 'Five of us, mate, can you get us in?' The Kingsway, in Southport, was a particularly popular spot. It had four floors of music, from the sixties to the nineties. I'd go with a few mates and we'd get free drinks all night, because having a Liverpool player around meant more people would want to get in. No doubt there'd have been drugs around in clubs at that time but that was never anything players were interested in. Even if we had been tempted, we got drug-tested all the time. I was selected after the FA Cup semi-final against Arsenal in 1993. Try having a piss after running round Wembley for ninety minutes on a boiling hot afternoon. It was an hour before I could produce a drop. The rest of the lads were on the coach and I still hadn't had a shower. After any game, you don't need a piss for four hours because you're so dehydrated – that's a fact. I was always baffled. Why the hell didn't they just do the test beforehand?

At Liverpool, when we let off steam, we really did let off steam every chance we got. The drinking that went on was phenomenal. Nights out often went international. After a Saturday game at Anfield it wasn't unusual for us to fly over to Dublin and get straight on it. Twenty-two minutes it took on the plane, I remember it clearly. They knew us so well at Liverpool Airport that we didn't even have to show our passports. Straight out onto the runway and that was that. Dublin was always another level. Someone would suggest it and the rest of us would be like, 'No! What did you say that for? You know what that means? We're going to have to do it now!' The intention was to come home Sunday morning. All too often though, we'd end up coming back on the first plane on Monday. We'd already have pissed our wives and partners off by going in the first place. With the damage done, our attitude was we might as well stay out there – in for a penny and all that. Not that I only did a disappearing act in Dublin. Not coming home was a longstanding habit of mine. My mind always worked in a weird way. If someone told me I needed to be home by midnight, I'd be back at 2 a.m. If someone told me

I could stay out half the night, I'd be back at eleven. I blame Jack Daniel's for those vanishing acts. Whenever I had a glass of that stuff at the end of a night it did something to me that meant I'd never go home and I'd just kick on. So blame Jack. Actually, I didn't call him Jack, I called him John because I knew him so well.

On other occasions we'd pile in a minibus straight round to Blackpool. Carnage every single time. But sometimes we'd venture no further than a couple of miles. At Tottenham after a game, it wasn't uncommon for us to go for a drink with the fans in the pubs near White Hart Lane, which was handy as I couldn't wait to get stuck into a pint. In fact, I was recently reminded that at Spurs after a game I'd have two on the way to the players' lounge. At Liverpool, meanwhile, if we'd won we'd find ourselves walking round town chatting and having a laugh with the same people who'd just watched us play from the stands. We didn't drink with fans because we thought we should. We did it because we liked it and they liked it back. It was a great feeling all round. That big separation between fans and players hadn't really happened yet. I'm not saying it was back to the days when players got a bus to the ground with their boots slung over one shoulder, but it was definitely more relaxed. It was like we knew everyone and they knew us.

If a famous footballer walked into a pub now, it'd be madness. Selfies with everyone. People filming it, putting it on social media. Word getting round and hundreds more heading down for a look. Go back thirty years and it was different. You'd get a bit of attention, but not like it is now. You were pretty much treated as a normal bloke. But then football was more normal then too. When I started playing for Liverpool, fans could stand on the Kop for less than a tenner. Nowadays a day out at the football for a couple of adults and two kids, with tickets, programmes and something to eat, would cost the same as a week in Benidorm. A lot of ordinary fans have been priced out of the game. Back in the day, they could rock up and watch us at the training ground. Now those places are like Fort Knox. Footballers are treated like film stars. I'm surprised they don't have a red carpet leading out onto the pitch.

Any player would be mad to go out round town if they'd got beat. We didn't lose at Anfield often, but when we did, and the immediate hurt and disappointment was wearing off, the thought would occur to us: 'Shit! We can't go out and get pissed now.' Tottenham was different. London's a big place. If there were places you couldn't go, there were still plenty more you could. Liverpool wasn't like that. You couldn't go anywhere without being clocked. I even had to go to Wigan, a rugby town, to do my shopping. Sometimes I'd head across to the Armani shop in Manchester. I'd be in hat, scarf and sunglasses, like a really bad undercover agent. I had to wear a disguise because there were people in Manchester who'd quite happily have chopped my bollocks off. Or worse – if there is worse.

I go to Manchester now and I get fans saying to me, 'Oh Razor, I used to love you!'

'No, you didn't,' I reply. 'You used to hate me.'

'Yes,' they say, 'but I love you now.'

I suppose it's progress. At least they don't want to throw darts at me anymore. In fact, a dart in the backside would have been a positive treat compared to what some fans, and not only of Man United, seemed to have in mind. I did actually get death threats. I got a bullet through the post with 'Ruddock' written on it. The police left my house with live ammunition. Other times I'd get notes, like people saying they knew where my kids went to school. Football can be a very weird place. Most people will leave it at a mouthful of abuse from the stands, or slag you off while they're in the pub with their mates, but there's always one or two who take their level of bile and hatred to a completely different level. I mean, who goes to the lengths of getting a bullet from somewhere and then carving a footballer's name on to it before sending it through the post? Yes, all sportspeople take what they do seriously. We're naturally competitive. We want to win. But at the end of the day it's a game, not a war.

Younger people especially are often amazed when I tell them about the boozing that used to go on in football. Nowadays, there's a generation who don't see alcohol in the same way. If they don't want to drink, that's fine. They'll say so and nobody will give them any grief for it. When I played, you did whatever the older players told you. I'm sure there'll be people who played Sunday football who'll recognise exactly the same dynamic in terms of the older lads putting the pressure on the younger ones to go out and get drunk. At Liverpool, it felt like if you didn't drink, you didn't play for the club. If the senior lads said, 'We're going out!' you did exactly that, because if you didn't you'd look weak, uncommitted and stupid. In an environment like a football dressing room, the last thing you wanted to do was stand out as somehow awkward or different. That was no fun. And anyway, how could you resist even if you wanted to? Which I most definitely didn't.

At Liverpool these people were my absolute heroes. I'd watched them as a kid winning European Cups, FA Cups, endlessly topping the league. Same as we have social media influencers now, they were the influencers of their day. And now here they all were. I was doing all right myself at that point. I'd proven that I could play the game. But nothing can ever prepare you for the moment you find yourself in that company as one of them. In my mind, they were massive. And in reality they *were* massive. True legends of the game. I didn't have to remind myself that it would be very easy to make a complete tit of myself in that situation. If I walked into that changing room for the first time looking all gormless, starstruck and barely able to get my words out, it would have been terrible. I did my best to be normal as I said hello – I don't remember wetting myself or anything like that – but inside I was melting. Just because you're a big character on the outside, doesn't necessarily mean you're the same on the in. I hung on their every word, and I definitely wasn't going to say no to anything they suggested. If they were going out on the lash, you went out on the lash. If they were chucking their car keys in the pot in a card game, you did the same. It was great, brilliant. There was no other way to look at it. Never for one minute did I look at anyone in a dressing room and think they were overdoing it, or, heaven forbid, might even have a problem. If anything it was the opposite. Wow! They're an amazing drinker! When I was coming through, older players would actually tell me, 'Work hard! The fitter you are, the more beer you can drink.' And they meant it.

When I became that older player myself, I hit the repeat button. At West Ham later in my career, I didn't want to hear someone say no when I suggested a night out, same as the senior players hadn't when I was the new kid on the block at Spurs and Liverpool. In that dressing room were incredible young players like Rio Ferdinand, Frank Lampard, Joe Cole, Michael Carrick and Jermain Defoe. They grew up in the same atmosphere I had a decade before – whatever the older players said, you did it. The difference at West Ham was that while they had a Tuesday club, by the time I left it was definitely on the wane. Attitudes began to change and it was made up of less and less people. The rule was that you just had to show your face rather than end up twelve hours down the line staggering to a taxi with a kebab in your hand. Paulo Di Canio, for instance, would turn up, have a diet Coke, and then go. To be fair, he didn't need alcohol to make him act like a madman. He was like that anyway. But it was important that everyone came along because it justified the Tuesday Club's existence. If it's just two of you propping up the bar, you can't really claim it's a team-building exercise. It's just getting pissed all day with your mate. Diluted it might have been, but the drinking culture was definitely still there at West Ham when I retired.

I don't want it to look like I'm getting on my high horse about booze in football. I don't expect players, or anybody else for that matter, not to go out and have fun. Totally the opposite in fact. As we all know, there's plenty of times when life deals you a bad hand, so when you get a few good cards you should go out and celebrate. There's nothing wrong with that. The difference now is that players feel comfortable and confident to celebrate whatever way they want. They also don't spend their days with alcohol brands emblazoned across their chests. When I then went to Tottenham, they were sponsored by Holsten. Liverpool? Carlsberg. What chance did I have? At Liverpool, when you won Man of the Match, you'd be given a crate of Carlsberg's extra-strong Elephant Beer. You simply cannot imagine that now. At least West Ham wasn't sponsored by a drinks manufacturer. They were sponsored by Dr Martens. (I wonder if they sponsored Millwall as well!)

Wherever you went, in and around football, booze was everything. Players, fans, we were all at it. Quite often when I was at Spurs my brothers would have seats in a box at White Hart Lane, call in at a pub round the corner on the way, and end up not even bothering going to the match. At least they hadn't come very far. The best I ever heard on that front was two of their mates who travelled all the way to Budapest to watch Millwall in what turned out to be their only ever game in Europe, and stayed drinking in a bar.

Ultimately, it was Arsene Wenger – him again – who changed the drinking culture in English football. He was the one who came in and told hardened English pros that the key to long-term success was looking after themselves properly, eating a good diet and cutting out the booze. He was the one who made people sit up and listen because he showed that treating players like athletes rather than workhorses got results. Changing players' mindsets meant changing something much bigger – the culture. Why has the drinking element drifted out of the game in the last ten to twenty years? For the very same reason it survived for so long – the younger players are following the example of the senior pros. If the best players in the team don't drink, then chances are the younger players won't either.

That change in culture really hit home for me after the 2005 Champions League Final when Liverpool came from three down to beat AC Milan in Istanbul. I saw a picture of the Liverpool players on the plane home after what would surely be the greatest game of their lives – and they were all drinking bottles of water. Unimaginable. I looked at that photo and thought, what happened to drinking champagne from the trophy? Or cracking open two dozen crates of beer (Istanbul to Liverpool is a three-and-a-half hour flight)? The dressing room culture had clearly changed massively in the seven years since I'd been there. I was amazed how a chain of behaviour that was so hard to break – that booze-laden lifestyle that had swallowed up me and so many other players in the eighties and nineties – had been pulled apart in pretty much no time at all. Maybe that drive for change was what a lot of players had been waiting for, it's just that previously, they never had a voice. Maybe mentally they hadn't wanted to go out. Maybe they'd got problems at home that needed sorting. Maybe those problems had a lot to do with going out and getting pissed in the first place. But because those senior players – me included – said they were going out, they went out.

Back in 2005, I'm sure I'd have told anyone who'd listen that by drinking water that Liverpool team was missing out on one of the most memorable nights of their lives. Actually, had they thrown a load of booze down themselves, it was more likely to be a memorable night they'd never remember. By ditching the drinking culture, they'd also never suffer the downwards career spiral that alcohol can shove you on. No matter what you do to weigh it off, excessive boozing affects your fitness. Which then means you don't get picked. Which then makes you feel more and more down. Which then makes you drink more. And so on and so on. That's exactly what happened to me. Deteriorating fitness meant I was getting bigger and bigger. I was playing less and less, which upset me, and so how did I deal with that? I drank until I forgot. Worse, I started drinking 'secretly' – with people who weren't going to report back to the club. Secrecy meant I could do it more and more. Hit the bottom of that helter-skelter and it's a long way back up.

6

THE DOWNWARD SLOPE

I expect there'll be one or two reading this book who'll think my reaction to being dropped for the 1996 FA Cup Final, the slide it put me on, is massively over the top. But maybe there'll have been a similarly devastating moment in their own life, when they've been overlooked for promotion, or a teacher's told them they're not good enough, or one of a million other types of rejection. Saying to someone who's hurt that they should just grow a pair and get over it totally misses the point. Wounds don't always leave a tidy scar. In my case, football – in particular achieving in football – was my life, and it always had been. It ruled everything I did. My family. Where I lived. Schools. Holidays. The list went on and on.

Liverpool was also my ideal club. My dream club. I loved it there. The fans were incredible. I defy any player not to feel ten foot tall playing in front of the Kop. Just hearing them sing is like an injection of adrenalin. 'You'll Never Walk

Alone' is the club's most famous song, of course, but 'Poor Scouser Tommy', about a young Liverpool fan dying on a foreign battlefield, is another that raises the hairs on the back of your neck. My favourite was one they dreamed up after I left, to the tune of 'The Runaway Train', for Fernando Torres:

> *His armband proved he was a red, Torres! Torres!*
> *You'll Never Walk Alone it said, Torres! Torres!*
> *We bought the lad from sunny Spain,*
> *He gets the ball he scores again,*
> *Fernando Torres! Liverpool's number 9!*

I won't mention the Carlos Tevez version the Liverpool fans used to sing when he was at Manchester United, other than to say I nearly fell off my seat laughing when I heard it.

Liverpool FC was the bubble wrap that kept the rest of my life from falling apart, but one by one those bubbles were being popped. Losing focus sparked a weight gain and dip in fitness. I knew I was carrying a little too much timber when I checked into a hotel in Regent's Park and was greeted by the bloke on reception: 'Nice to meet you, Mr Molby.' Jan Molby was known for being, shall we say, a little on the larger side. On the plus side, he was also very cool. I never checked, but word was he shat ice cubes.

Thing is, it's not just physically that you carry weight, you carry it mentally as well. You know you're not in the game like you should be. You're angry with yourself, frustrated, carrying that bit of self-loathing and guilt. You might have your own fans on your back as well. A couple of bad games and the mutters, murmurs and occasional shouts get worse. You start thinking, 'Hang on a minute, I'm not used to this. I'm the one everyone used to like.' But they stop liking you because you're now three feet away from that tackle you'd otherwise have put in. You haven't quite got the pace to get you into position to score that header.

Away fans having a go didn't bother me. If anything, I loved it. It just made me want to piss them off twice as bad by showing what I could do on the pitch to hurt them. Terry Venables taught me that lesson. One time with Tottenham I was playing away at Sheffield Wednesday. Their fans were absolutely caning me. We won, but afterwards I must have been looking pretty fed up in the changing room. Terry came over: 'What's up with you?'

'It's pissing me off,' I explained. 'Every away game, I get booed.'

He looked at me. 'Yes, son,' he replied, 'because you're a threat. If you were a nobody they'd take no notice of you.'

From that point on, every away game I'd do something to wind the home fans up. If someone shouted some abuse, for instance, I'd give them a bit back. I wanted to get booed. I loved it. 'This is what I'm here for!' It took the pressure off everyone else and made me feel good. But home fans having a go was totally different – something I never experienced before that Cup Final. Ask anyone who's ever played for Liverpool and they'll say the crowd is always fair. On the odd occasion we got beat at Anfield they never booed us off, same as sometimes they'd clap the team that beat us. It has to be one of the greatest places on earth to play football. But occasionally I would hear the odd comment coming in my direction. Inside, I wanted to play like I'd always done – to be that player they loved. *I'll show you!* But constant injuries made that impossible. I've heard people say that Londoners (I qualify since I was born there) don't fit in at Liverpool, but I never felt any animosity from Liverpool fans because of that. Actually I've always thought that Cockneys and Scousers have a lot in common. Similar sense of humour, quick-witted, family-orientated, always get a bad rap and no grasses! I always felt like it was home from home up there. Some of the Liverpool crowd grew frustrated with me – it's as simple as that. And in doing so they were only mirroring my own self-doubt.

When West Ham came in for me, I was still very much carrying that feeling. I couldn't get rid of it. I would constantly compare myself to how I was before. That meant both my performance and my confidence. It makes me laugh when the fixture list comes out and you hear a high-profile player say how they can't wait for Liverpool away or Man United. When I hear that, I always think, 'You lying bastard!' Because I know full well the games I always looked for were more like Coventry, Charlton or Ipswich at home. Man United away? That's going to be a nightmare! But now it felt like no game offered an easy ride. Remember also that the Premier League was strong from the start and then got stronger year by year. People think the big-name overseas strikers only really properly came into the Premier League in the last twenty years, but I was up against players like Thierry Henry, Gianfranco Zola and Dennis Bergkamp. A poor performance meant I'd be panned by fans and media alike. I hear some players say they're not aware of fans. I don't know if that's true or not, but grief from your own supporters can definitely affect you, put you off your game. Have a bad game. What do you do? Go out and have a drink. And so on.

Thing is, once you start going downhill it's like you're on skis, on the black run, with the slope getting steeper and steeper. There's no way you're getting back to the top. I see it happening to players all the time. Look at Jesse Lingard signing for a club in South Korea when only three years ago he was playing a big role for England, or Dele Alli turning out for a club in Turkey, having been maybe the best 21-year-old in the world. Players say the things their employers want to hear – 'It's great to be here. I can't wait to get out on the pitch' – but going from experience I can't help but wonder what's really going through their minds. It would be wrong to compare heading to West Ham with going to South Korea. West Ham is a big club, a great club, one with passionate support and great tradition. But it was obvious to anyone that my days vying for the top honours were gone. I made joining the Hammers work for me by seeing it as a chance of a new adventure and to come back home while still playing top-class football. I'd be nearer my mates who I grew up with and my dad would only have to travel half an hour to watch me play. Add up the little things and sometimes they make a lot.

I get it, in footballing terms, West Ham isn't Liverpool. But being there made me happy in terms of how I was going to live my life. Make no mistake, Liverpool had imploded for me after the Cup Final. I still loved the club but my relationship with it as a player had changed. I wouldn't say I was happy to get away but at the same time staying was a recipe for more and more disappointment and grief. At West Ham, I found another club to fall in love with, one where I felt valued, contented, part of a plan, and in Harry Redknapp had a manager who understood how players think and operate. I was on the slope, but it was still relatively even. In fact, you could actually argue it was upwards.

The first year I was at West Ham we finished fifth in the league, two places above Liverpool, and qualified for Europe for the first time in nearly two decades. I had a blast, as a player – and as a bad influence. Harry specifically told me he'd signed me to look after the youngsters. Within a matter of weeks I'd corrupted the lot of them. But while my methods were a little unorthodox, they were actually pretty much in line with what Harry wanted. He brought in older heads like me, Ian Wright, Stuart Pearce, Nigel Winterburn, Ray Parlour and Paolo Di Canio to teach the younger players how to handle themselves as footballers – so act like a gentleman, be good to people around you, and even, if and when the time's right, have a bit of fun and get to know one another by going out on the piss. Of course, I was at the other end of the track, and, happy or not, was increasingly finding myself sidelined by injuries that seemed harder and harder to shake off. A hamstring tear was a particular nightmare. I should have just taken time out and sorted it out, but I was scared, not of the surgery, but of being away from the rest of the lads, of my own company. Looking back, that should have been a warning sign. The end of my career was looming – and then I would have long days to fill away from the dressing room atmosphere that had been my reason to get up in the morning for so long.

As a footballer, being born in May means you're either going to have a bloody great birthday (promotion, a cup win), or a bad one (relegation, losing a final, or, worst of all, being dropped for it). This time, I'd just turned 30 when Harry called me into his office and told me I was on my way to Crystal Palace, a league lower in what was then termed the First Division. I neither resented his decision nor blamed him for it. Moving me on made good sense. To use horsing parlance, in Rio Ferdinand they had a prime thoroughbred. I, on the other hand, wasn't far off ending up in the knacker's yard.

Soon after I joined Crystal Palace, I had another sharp jab in the ribs that the end was nigh. I noticed a distinct mental switch, from *wanting* to go to training in the morning to *having* to go to training in the morning. Football, the absolute joy of my life, had suddenly become work. And in sport, once you feel like that, it's over. You're no longer what you've always thought you were. You're just hanging on in there because you don't know what else to do. You want it to end, but you don't want it to end. That mental shift isn't something you can easily hide from. For a start there's an unavoidable ingredient in the mix – the day-to-day gets physically harder. My body had definitely started complaining – 'Razor, have a look! Your knees are knackered, you can't run like you used to, your turning circle is like an oil tanker, and you can't get back to your ideal weight. Do us both a favour and fuck off and open a newsagent's.' When it comes to the verbals, your body really doesn't hold back. Although, to be fair, considering I'd spent year after year putting it through all kinds of twists, turns, knocks and collisions, the bollocking it gave me was actually pretty restrained.

In all honesty, I'd hoped to see out my playing days, nursing those knackered knees through as many appearances as possible at West Ham. When Palace came in it felt like I had to start all over again, which meant drawing on energy which seemed to have refused to make the trip with me from Upton Park. There was something else bothering me. I didn't know anyone at Palace, but of course they knew me. Or rather they knew Razor. That meant a problem. I'd arrive at that club as something I didn't particularly want to be anymore. People, I thought, would expect certain things of me – Razor being the main one of them.

It was when Palace gave me my shirt for my debut that I got the feeling Selhurst Park would be a very different kind of experience to what I'd been used to. I was on the bench. Or at least I was supposed to be on the bench. When Steve Coppell, the gaffer, turned round to signal for me to get ready to go on I was nowhere to be seen.

Coppell turned to his assistant Brian 'Spadge' Sparrow: 'Where is he?'

'Razor? He's in the dressing room, boss. He's refusing to come out.'

Thing is, when I say Palace gave me my shirt, I mean they gave me the shirt, the actual shirt, that had belonged to the player before me who'd just been sold on – a young kid, lithe, skinny, the sort who falls down cattle grids. Now I was quite a big lad at that point. Not Swindon big (as we'll see), but still big. The shirt was about a third my size. It was up around my armpits. Professional footballer? I looked more like a Bella Emberg tribute act. Then there were the shorts. I won't go into detail other than to say it looked like I'd shoplifted the last two lemons in Sainsbury's.

Coppell, unimpressed by my absence, despatched Spadge to fetch me. After a short period of negotiation, a compromise was reached. Yes, I'd come out, but only on the strict understanding I wasn't to be put on. The deal agreed, I ripped the strip off and went out in a tracksuit. Even if an emergency had happened and I'd had to go on, I'd rather have played in my birthday suit than that outfit.

To be fair, the first six months at Palace were great. I was captain, I was playing and, eventually, I had a shirt that fitted. And then I fell out with the chairman over a contractual matter. I wasn't having that. I had it out with him – I mean proper had it out, both of us effing and blinding at each other. It became a real battle, both sides hunkering down on their position. In the end I had to train with the kids and even on my own. But as long as I turned up good as gold at 10 o'clock for training every day there was nothing they could do. That was fine, but looking back, being isolated was probably the last thing I needed for my mental health. When you're already on a downwards spiral, being alone with your negative thoughts is never a good idea.

A saviour came in the form of Lee Hanning, manager of the Crystal Palace training ground. At a time when my relationship with the club was at a low, and with my personal life falling to pieces, his office became a proper little sanctuary. Unusually for a training ground manager, Lee went to the Sylvia Young Theatre School – he was actually in *Grange Hill* – and one of the things a theatre education had drummed into him was always to treat people – actors, singers, whoever – normally. When he started working at Palace he took that attitude with him and it worked perfectly. From the start he treated me not as a footballer but as a mate and I found I could talk to him about anything. On a nice day we'd have a game of golf on the tennis courts. Other times, when the clock struck eleven, we'd nip to O'Neill's round the corner for a couple of Guinnesses. I'd go home and Lee would go back to the training ground and attempt to do some work.

Lee often jokes about never meeting your heroes – because he met his and it ruined his life! But while I might not have done much for his productivity, he gave me loads of invaluable advice about how to take care of myself financially and would become an absolute rock during the long years of the divorce and its aftermath. He was like a guide to the real world, the one that I had no clue how to negotiate by myself. He was there for me whatever time of day or night, never telling me what he thought I wanted to hear but telling me the truth. I needed that in my life – it's something that people don't always do. I often get asked who my biggest mates in football are, but actually I wouldn't say I have many really close friends in the game. Don't get me wrong, there are players who I meet up with and have a laugh with, but really deep friendships? That's something else. Football's like that – people come and people go. You can be friends with a player one minute and then not see them again for fifteen years. It's the friends I've made outside football who I've always stayed close to. My brothers are my best mates, pals from school. Those friendships are built on that bit of honesty. It's not really a friendship if you don't say what you really feel.

There was another thing about Lee. As an actor himself he could see the actor in me. I might not have been to drama school but I'd been playing Razor for years. He watched how in any situation I'd always try to have a laugh and a joke – sometimes barely able to get the words out quick enough – and see it for the defence mechanism it obviously was. When you lack confidence, when your self-esteem has taken a battering, you put up a barrier, and humour was mine. I've always been quick-witted enough to do that. When you think about it, there's not many of us who aren't actors. Every time someone comes up to us and says, 'Hi mate, how are you?'

and we reply, 'Yeah, great. No problem', chances are we're acting. Easier to pretend than tell the truth.

Later, I found the same close friendship out of nowhere with Rylan Clark, the *X Factor* star who I shared the *Celebrity Big Brother* house with in 2013. Fellow smokers, we were forever stood chatting with one another and I liked him straightaway, especially his openness. He'd dealt with a lot in life, been bullied at school, and there was a naivete about him which didn't quite fit in with the cut-throat entertainment business he found himself in. He showed his honesty and strength when he dealt with his own mental health crisis and tried to help others by talking about it. Both Lee and Rylan had starring roles at mine and Leah's wedding. Lee was my best man while Rylan was the ringbearer. We've remained great mates, which is how I got away with buying him a horse file for his teeth on his 30th birthday.

In the end, Simon Jordan paid me to leave Palace. I didn't show it, but underneath I was delighted to walk away. Those last few months at the club had taught me for certain that I didn't want to be a footballer anymore. Mentally and physically it had become too hard. I was never going to say that out loud, but it was the truth. In the years since, I've met

Simon several times on talkSPORT. These days we have a different sort of conversation. We've both realised that mentally at Palace I wasn't in a good place. But whatever it was I had – mental health issues, depression, or whatever – hadn't been invented then. He didn't know what I was going through and I didn't know how to talk about any of that stuff anyway. Maybe if we'd had that knowledge we'd have had a different kind of conversation. And to be fair to Simon, when all's said and done my head wasn't right and I was a spoiled footballer. When you're like that you think everything is someone else's fault and not your own.

Whatever the ins and outs of it, one thing was for sure – I was ready to get away from Palace. By that stage I couldn't train hard even if I'd wanted to. If my legs were in the mood, my brain wasn't or vice-versa. Trying to be Razor with a head full of self-doubt and zero confidence was difficult in the extreme. I still tried to be the life and soul but nothing felt quite the same. I was getting older so my body was suffering, I was getting up feeling tired, my homelife was a mess, and then I had to drive an hour-and-a-half through London traffic every day. I challenge anyone to arrive at work with a smile on their face when life's taken a turn like that. When you've got to drag yourself out of bed feeling like crap every day, it's a big ask to stick a grin on and run around. But still you try.

You don't have to be a footballer to feel like that. There'll be plenty of people whose heads are on the floor but have to sit behind a desk every day and look happy. The unfortunate reality of being in that situation is the more you do it, the worse you feel. I spent so many training sessions pretending to be someone, and something, I wasn't. But, like anyone in any job will testify, the hardest thing to do is face up to the issue and walk out the door. Trying again somewhere else, or at something else, just doesn't feel like an option. It's a hurdle that's fifty feet tall.

Razor certainly wasn't something I felt able to walk away from. If you're the one giving it the big 'un in the changing room, and then suddenly you stop because you feel shit about yourself, then you're putting a massive question mark above your head. What's up with him? He's never like that. He's changed. He's no fun. He's gone. Razor didn't have an off button or airplane mode. Even though a lot of the time at Palace I was half Razor – Razor with a blunt edge – I was still on. Good thing for Palace that I was. The club had a bad run and were in serious danger of getting relegated. My answer was to bring the lads together, have a few good nights out and bring a few smiles to the place. With a few drinks in me I could also switch up to proper Razor, that big presence that I couldn't quite summon up elsewhere. While Simon Jordan wasn't too impressed with me taking the players out on the piss – he accused me of getting them wasted when we were fighting relegation – truth was it worked. A team destined for the drop into the third tier stayed up. And it does make you wonder what Jordan thought he was going to get if he wasn't happy with me going down the pub with the players. I'd been doing it for nearly twenty years by then, it might as well have been in the contract.

Those drink-ups were another indication to me that however I might be feeling on the inside, Razor could be raised from the dead with a few beers. My relationship with food was also beginning to change. I had a clause at Palace stating I had to weigh less than 15 stone. Violate it and I'd be fined. But food gave me comfort when I was down. It was like getting out of a freezing cold pool and wrapping myself in a thick warm towel. If it was a choice between a fine and a curry, I'd be sat in that curry house every time. The *Metro* once did a piece about 'the top ten largest Crystal Palace players ever'. Guess who was number one? Although you're not telling me they didn't have some Fatty Arbuckle-esque goalkeeper in the past – every club had one of them.

I really should have walked away from football after Palace. Instead I went to Swindon as player/coach alongside my old Liverpool boss, Roy Evans. On arrival, I thought no way could that Palace debacle with my kit happen again. And then, blow me, it turned out they didn't have a pair of shorts that fitted me in the entire place – kit store, club shop, any-where. An SOS had to be sent out to their kit manufacturers. It might have been better for all concerned if they'd never found a pair and I'd just gone home – Swindon really was a case of a club too far. There's a photo on my wall of me at the Robins. I'm overweight, I'm knackered, and I've been sent off. It was 21 December 2001 – Happy Christmas! Not that I gave a fuck. When the ref showed me that red card I was already gone. Not just from the pitch but from football.

That's a 100 per cent honest summary of how I felt. I could sit here and say that I was happy as my career slowly came to an end, that it was just as good to play for Palace and Swindon as it was for Spurs and Liverpool, but I'd be telling lies. I'd played for some great clubs which I felt a real affinity to, whereas Palace felt like the last stop on the track. Fantastic club, great fans and a superb crop of young players at that time, but for me, physically, and in the head, I was done. I'd run out in front of massive crowds at White Hart Lane and Anfield. I'd had thousands and thousands of people singing my name. I'd felt a hundred foot tall. Lived a dream. Had a heart bursting with pride at what I'd achieved. I don't care what anyone says, it's a terrible feeling when that bubble bursts. It was like being MD at Marks & Spencer and ending up stacking shelves at Lidl. Players try and try to get back what they've lost but it never works. In many ways, they're tricked by what they do. In sport, the good days are never that long ago. What they forget is the end is also never that far away. I always joke that later in my career when I'd look at the player ratings in the match reports in the Sunday papers I'd get annoyed because they kept spelling my name as 'Ruddocks'. Then I realised it was actually 'Ruddock 5'. Like I say, a joke, but there's a serious point at the heart of it – the time comes when you can never be what you once were. You don't need to be a Premier League footballer to experience that slide, to feel like the future you had all planned out is slipping out of control. It's happening right now to hundreds of thousands of people across all areas of life. Chances are it's happening to people you know and love. Many of them will just be hanging in there for the day they can draw their pension. Pro-footballers are different only in that they get their pension when they're 35, a saviour for many, because when you're a kid and someone tells you, 'Save this, save that,' chances are you never listened to a word they were saying.

People often ask me as a footballer if I have regrets. My reply is always the same: I don't have regrets, I just have good and bad experiences. I always tried my hardest. I was always told, 'Every game you give your best'. And I believed in that. Doing your best means that if bad times come you can look back and think, 'I couldn't have done anything about it.' Only if you could have tried harder and changed what happened will you have regrets. Fans of whatever club, whether I played for them or not, respected me because when I crossed that white line I did always give my best. Football fans aren't stupid. They can see if someone isn't working hard, or hiding from the ball. Being brave in football doesn't mean going around hurting people, it means always wanting the ball, always wanting to try something. Fans understand players and their motivation. They saw my motivation was always to do my best and that's why I was liked wherever I went.

Being a footballer is a great job, but it's one of the hardest as well. Yes, you're living a dream, but, like all dreams, it's one you have pretty much no control over. Same goes for the money and lifestyle. Fantastic, but the weight that comes with it is immense. Your own fans are on your side, but they make up about 0.001 per cent of the population. Everyone else is hoping you bollocks it up. And then a few days later you've got to go out there and do it all again. Meanwhile, you might have to move your entire family to the other end of the country at a moment's notice and start over somewhere completely new.

And yet, while I had plenty of ups and downs in the game, the problem for me was never being a footballer. The problem for me was *not* being a footballer. Because while I might have been ready to step away from the game, I couldn't work out what it was I was stepping into. Football – busy, sociable, all-consuming football – was my comfort zone. I had no idea how I was going to live in a world without it. No idea quite how traumatic that rebirth was going to be. I was Razor, and I was screwed.

7

EMPTY

It's the loneliness that gets you.

Going from the biggest, most fun, environment you could ever have to sitting on your own. Of course, all good things come to an end. Question is, what happens then? In an ideal world, as I neared the end of my career, there'd have been someone there to prepare me for the transition: 'You'll be retired in a year's time, Razor, these are the things you need to think about.' That help is there in football now. Twenty years ago, it was totally absent. All I had was me. And I wasn't exactly multi-skilled. Like most footballers I'd been lucky enough to sail through life without ever having a proper job. And anyway I'd done well out of the game, I didn't need a job. Which then leaves you with a lot of time on your hands. Maybe if your marriage has survived your career, then you throw yourself into family life. Mine wasn't so much on the rocks as sunk without trace.

It isn't just purpose that's missing, there's other gaping holes to contend with. That incredible buzz, the one you get when you come off the pitch having won, is gone – from hero to zero in the blink of an eye. And those thirty lads you used to spend half your life with have gone too. You don't think about it so much at the time but that bond is really intense. As a squad you're totally reliant on one another. Everything you do, everything you are, is dependent on the person next to you. If the team is winning then everything runs smoothly. If it isn't, inevitably that's when things fall apart. Together, once, often twice, a week you have to try to get over the line in first position. Sport is a workplace like no other because it is so results driven. Sharing that pressure is vital and you do that through unity. Everything is about being as one. I mean, how many workplaces do you know where everyone jumps naked into a giant bath at the end of the day? Something I loved by the way, so long as I wasn't last in. By then it was like a Pot Noodle. Stuff floating round all over the place. You were basically washing your face in (at best) a soup of mud, sweat, piss, toenails and pubes. That was the best thing about getting sent off – you were first in the bath. You could spend half an hour wallowing in there before anyone else arrived.

While times have moved on and clubs don't tend to have the communal bath anymore, every footballer remains dependent on the dressing room and the bond it delivers. When retirement comes you'll do anything to replace what you've lost, and all too often the obvious place to look is the pub. After all, with the laughter, the banter, the stupid arguments, what's a dressing room but a pub without the drink? Of course, actually it's nowhere near the same. A dressing room is a professional environment, a gateway to personal satisfaction and achievement. A pub is somewhere you go to get pissed. I knew that, but in my mind it was all I had.

I'd already done the whole going out and playing golf every day thing, but after a month of that all I could think was, 'Jesus, this is boring' and that's why, sat at home twiddling my thumbs at 11 o'clock one Tuesday morning, I began to wonder where I could best find that matchday buzz in my new non-football life. 'I know,' I thought, 'Wetherspoons!' I'd walked past there at half ten in the morning and seen fellas in the window having a pint and a fry-up. It was the perfect place to make some new mates. And so Wetherspoons it was. Over time, I got to know a new crowd of people. Tuesdays and Thursdays they'd be in Wetherspoons, Wednesdays and Fridays a different boozer, and so on. Soon enough I'd moved on from that old Tuesday Club that existed in football to having a Tuesday Club every day of the week. One big session would run straight into another. I'd stay out for days on end, each time waking up feeling like shit. 'I'm not doing that again,' I'd think, and then half an hour later I'd be back outside some pub or other, waiting for the doors to open.

Naturally, I wouldn't be living that life as myself. I'd leave Neil in front of the shaving mirror. Razor was the man for the pub, a constant companion, an alcohol-fuelled alter ego I was becoming more and more dependent on at the most destructive time of my life. After all, when you're drunk it deals with everything. Like I say, mad, bad, sad, glad – you're the happiest man in the world again. At least that's what you tell yourself. If Neil was lost and miserable, Razor was the man to make the good times roll. Hiding behind someone I wasn't should have rung every alarm bell in my head, but I was in a bad place mentally, hopeless and lonely, and back then you didn't question your behaviour. It's only in recent times that men have been encouraged to look at the direction they're heading and ask if they're going the right way.

Looking back, I must have appeared quite a tragic figure. Sometimes in the pub I wouldn't know anyone. That was when I'd have to 'kidnap' someone at the bar with the promise that I'd pay for their drinks. Some poor sod would go out for an innocent pint and be missing for a week. But these people would tell me what I wanted to hear: 'You're the greatest, Razor! You're a legend.' I was insecure away from football and needed people like that around me. But they're not the ones you really need when you're damaging yourself, because they're never going to tell you the truth. They're never going to say, 'Come on, mate! Pull yourself together! This ain't going to help.' They're just happy to be out on the piss with someone who used to be a bit of a face and is paying for them to drink all day and all night. I'd wake up the next day and not even know their names. They were just stepping stones that allowed me to get to where I wanted – oblivion. I dread to think how many people there are out there who've said to their mates, 'Guess who I was out with last night? Razor Ruddock!' I hope you enjoyed yourselves because I don't remember any of it.

I wasn't alone in trying to find a lost world in the pub. You hear so many ex-footballers of my era say how they were banging on the door at 11 a.m. They weren't doing that just because they wanted a drink. What they really wanted was a portal into a lost world. When you go from football to nothing it's like part of you dies. You don't want to watch football, you don't want to watch your team play and you don't want to read the papers. No-one ever, ever, has told you how to deal with that. Drinking is the only way you know to handle anything that hurts. But you soon realise you're chasing something impossible. Alcohol can never replace that feeling. Sitting at the bar in a pub all day can never be the same as fighting to win a game of football with your mates and the sense of togetherness that comes with it. Some players try to fill the void by taking ambassador roles at their former clubs. I thought about doing the same but I was still young and didn't want to walk back into White Hart Lane or Anfield and take a more senior ex-player's job. For a lot of ex-pros, it's a big part of their life and I respected that.

The sudden absence of the discipline that's ruled your life only makes matters worse. For years you've been told where to be, what to do, what to wear, who to deal with. You've lived under two bosses – your manager and your wife. When you retire, you still (maybe, just about) have your wife but the attitude then is, 'I'm not listening to her.' I know that sounds bad, but that's what we footballers do. Chances are we'll have been doing it for years – letting the family down but never letting our mates down. When you're drinking every night you don't think you're doing anything wrong. You look at other people and think, 'Well hang on, they're doing it, why shouldn't I?' The difference is those people go home. They accept their responsibilities. We're the 1 per cent whose outlook has twisted the opposite way. These days I've completely changed. I don't give a monkey's what anyone says to me, I won't let the wife and kids down. But it's taken me till now to get like that. And I'm lucky that Leah came along and gave me a second chance at family life.

It sounds so outdated but, like a lot of other lads, I was married by the age of 20. At that time, marrying young was a thing, as everyone reckoned it would calm a bloke down. I don't think that quite worked with me, but being a professional footballer as a teenager and married so soon did mean I missed out on a lot of everyday experiences that 'normal' people had. I never went to Benidorm with the lads, stayed up all weekend, all that kind of stuff. Not the end of the world, I know. I was hardly deprived. But it did mean that when I retired, there were things still rattling around in me that might otherwise have gone. And I think that's a big reason why my last dregs of discipline went and like some terrible Hollywood movie I turned straight back into an 18-year-old. I'd lived with the constant requirement for at least some degree of restraint, and then overnight it had gone. It was like being set free into the world again, like when you're walking your dog and it disappears the second you let it off the leash. No restrictions. I could do whatever I wanted – and that's exactly what I did.

Plenty of footballers end up divorced within a year of retirement and I can totally understand it. But in all probability that relationship was sunk long ago. Even the strongest marriage would do well to survive the big fuck-off iceberg that football sticks right in the middle of the ocean. Take that ultimate in family time, Christmas. For me, the day itself meant opening presents at 7 a.m. with the kids then heading off to training. If we were playing away, I wouldn't be back until Boxing Day night. If it was a home game, I'd be back for Christmas dinner but couldn't have any. Half a turkey, a dozen pigs in blankets and a Christmas pudding smeared in custard? Next day you might as well run out on to the pitch in a Victorian diving suit. On 27 December, I'd be back at training, getting ready for the next game, which might be twenty-four hours later.

Of course, footballers do get a summer break. But I'd finish the season in May, have June off, and by the time the kids broke up, I'd be back in pre-season training ready to get going again in August. Everyone thinks you're in a villa for three months having a great time with your kids when the truth is they're at school all the time. The best you can hope for is a long weekend on a bank holiday. Whatever the reason for the collapse, when the end comes, you find that in no time at all you've gone from two bosses, to one, to no bosses at all. On the face of it, you can do what you want, when you want. But no-one lives in isolation. There will always be other people involved who get hurt.

Without guidance and support, the vast majority of players haven't got a clue how to live a non-footballing life. At 16, the game classifies you as an adult but you're nothing of the sort. How can you be when so much is done for you? You live in a bubble that can last from ten to twenty years. When I came out of football I didn't know how to get through an airport on my own, how to book a doctor's appointment, anything. I'd been institutionalised by football. Sounds mad, but you really are that far removed from everyday life. You don't even know who you are anymore. I mean literally who you are. For as long as I could remember I'd been Neil 'Razor' Ruddock, the footballer. Who the hell was I now? I was back on Civvy Street with everyone else. I just happened to have played football. That was the only lifeline I had to cling on to. The problem was, holding the other end of the rope was Razor. Without him, I faced catastrophe. Let go of that rope and I was gone. At least that's how it felt. It was a hell of a lot easier to rely on Razor than to face a leap into the unknown as Neil. There was no-one there with a safety net. My marriage was a wreck and the protective shell of the dressing room was gone. Razor was all I had. I'd gone from being around a packed little dressing room to a big empty house. There was no help to make that transition. When football doesn't need you anymore that's the end of it. And so instead I went to the pub and stayed there all day and every day. Get smashed, get even more smashed, and do it all over again. What starts out as a few days' boozing after you've retired, just to enjoy what you've been missing out on, soon turns into weeks and then months. I was thinking about this the other day. Did I need the social life? Or did I need the drink? In the end, I concluded it was both. It had to be. The drink brought Razor to life, and Razor was the catalyst for something like a social life.

As a last attempt at saving my marriage I agreed to check into rehab at Tony Adams' Sporting Chance Clinic, the Professional Footballers' Association (PFA) helping out with the cost. Tony was one of the first players to open up about alcoholism and addiction. His own drinking had resulted in a four-month prison sentence after he crashed his car into a wall while four times over the drink-drive limit. He wanted to help make sure others didn't end up the same way, providing a wide range of support to current and former sportspeople for all sorts of mental health problems. Sounds a great idea – until it's you who's being booked in. My initial reaction was a classic for blokes like me: 'What do I want to do that for? How's that going to help? Leave it out. These people know nothing about me.' I felt really uncomfortable about the idea. I'd grown up in a world where people talked about 'nutters' going to 'the loony bin' and now it felt like that 'nutter' was me. Pulling up outside, one thought dominated my mind: 'I don't belong here.' At the same time I couldn't help thinking what people had said to me on so many occasions, on and off the pitch: 'You're mad you are, Razor – mad!' Sitting in the car, something began to nag at the back of my mind: 'Maybe I am mad. Maybe they actually meant it.'

The clinic was at the back of Champneys, the Hampshire spa and hotel where George Best used to stay. It wasn't quite the same level of pampered luxury. Sporting Chance operated a fixed regime that everyone had to stick to. That was made clear with a bag search on entry, making sure you weren't bringing in booze, drugs, 300 Mars Bars, or whatever. You could have your fags but that was it. Health was the order of the day.

From that point on you weren't allowed off the premises. I'd come to Sporting Chance after my stint in the jungle on *I'm a Celebrity . . .* The show isn't easy. While as a footballer I was used to being thrown into a group of strangers who were expected to act as a team, after three days I was so tired I just wanted to be left alone. A jungle rat the size of a cat would appear by my bed and instead of screaming I'd just think, 'Bite me, fuck off, and leave me be.' The Sex Pistols singer John Lydon was a saviour for me. I found him fascinating and would listen to him talking about all kinds of stuff for hours. Then, when the cameras were on him, he'd turn into Johnny Rotten. Razor times ten. If I had problems with Razor, the personality shift between John Lydon and Johnny Rotten was on another planet. While the time passed slowly, it was a buzz being involved in such a big show, and when I left the camp, walking out over that familiar rope bridge, I felt like I was famous all over again. My response to that was 100 per cent predictable. Get madder. And madder. And madder. My drinking, my staying out for days on end, got totally out of hand. Checking into Sporting Chance soon had me wishing I'd stayed in the jungle. A month with spiders and snakes would have been a lot easier.

(above) Birth certificate – no messing about with middle names.

(above, right) At my mother's knee. I was lovely as a baby – I couldn't answer back.

(right) Angelic – I could have been a choir boy. Maybe not!

(below, left) Football mad – I loved playing for St Thomas More.

(below, right) Sporting the 1982 England football kit – striker Kevin Keegan was my hero.

(above) With brothers Gary (left) and Colin (right). I soon caught up to them!

(right) It was either football or modelling for the Littlewoods catalogue.

(left) 'Could you please report for Pre-Season Training at the Den' – don't mind if I do!

(below) A dream moment – joining Millwall and becoming a pro.

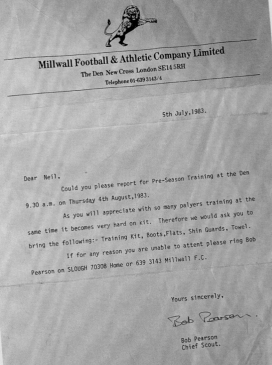

Millwall Football & Athletic Company Limited
The Den New Cross London SE14 5RH
Telephone 01-639 3143/4

5th July, 1983.

Dear Neil,
Could you please report for Pre-Season Training at the Den 9.30 a.m. on Thursday 4th August, 1983.
As you will appreciate with so many palyers training at the same time it becomes very hard on kit. Therefore we would ask you to bring the following:- Training Kit, Boots, Flats, Shin Guards, Towel.
If for any reason you are unable to attent please ring Bob Pearson on SLOUGH 70308 Home or 639 3143 Millwall F.C.

Yours sincerely,

Bob Pearson

Bob Pearson
Chief Scout.

Directors A.A. THORNE Chairman H.T.J. BURNIGE F.R.I.C.S. W.J. NELAN B.A. THORNE
Manager: GEORGE GRAHAM Secretary: G.P. HOVER

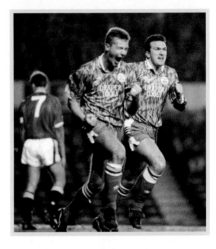

(*above, left*) Spurs was my ideal club – ground, history, kit – an incredible move for me at just 17 years old.

(*above, right*) Wrestling with Peter Beardsley. One of my first acts at Liverpool was to break his cheekbone.

(*right*) Celebrating at Old Trafford with my pal Alan Shearer, fully recovered after I nearly cut off his toes.

(*below, left*) Back to Spurs. Terry Venables would have taken us to greatness – if he'd been allowed.

(*below, right*) My England cap against Nigeria was a proud moment.

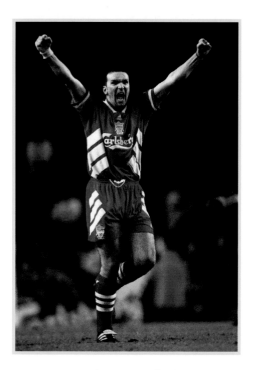

(*above, left*) Playing for Liverpool was a fantasy come true.

(*above, right*) Full time at Wembley against Bolton and the Ruddock Stomp makes a return.

(*below, left*) Winning the Coca-Cola Cup with Liverpool was a great moment . . .

(*below, right*) . . . but nothing could ever make up for being dropped for the FA Cup Final.

(right)
Patrick Vieira committed one of the biggest no-nos in football when he spat in my face.

(left) Battling for the ball against Davor Šuker during the West Ham v Arsenal FA Carling Premiership game, 1999.

(right) The end was nigh – playing for Crystal Palace.

(left) Ian Wright was always on my back!

(below) I'm A Celebrity . . . Get Me Out Of Here! – where I started smoking aged 35!

(left) Celebrity Big Brother – the only thing that saved the experience was becoming pals with Rylan Clark

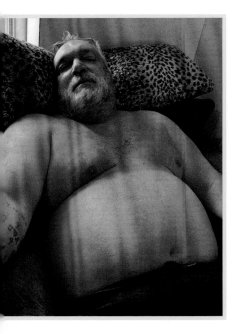

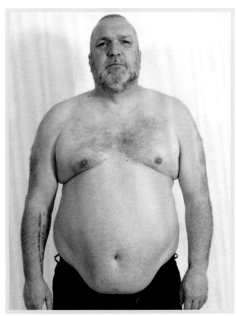

(above) Looking back now it's hard to believe how big I got. Without drastic change, death was round the corner.

(below, left) Gastric sleeve surgery – I'll never forget how an incredible medical team made it so, so easy.

(below, right) The new me. Literally half the man I used to be.

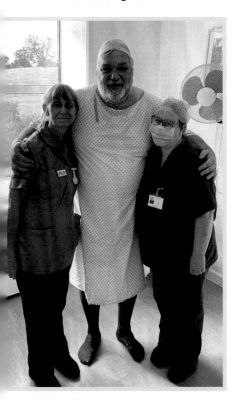

(above) Healthy in mind and body, I can be the dad to Pebbles and Kizzy I want to be.

(below) My beautiful wife Leah – she saved me from myself.

That month included thirty Alcoholics Anonymous meetings in thirty days. At the first one I got up: 'Hi, my name's Neil and I'm an alcoholic.' It never occurred to me to call myself Razor. Maybe I should have done since he was at the root of a lot of the bad habits and behaviour that had put me there, but I hadn't taken that in yet. I'll be straight – when I stood up and spoke those words, I didn't believe a word I was saying. They'd diagnosed me as a 'binge alcoholic' – someone who really goes for it with the aim of getting totally off their head as quickly as possible. Since that was exactly what I'd been doing for years and years it was hard to argue with the diagnosis, the binging side anyway. I was 100 per cent a binge drinker. But then again so was pretty much everyone else in those days. You went out to get pissed, especially as a footballer, because you couldn't go out recreationally whenever you liked. If I was an alcoholic then pretty much everyone else who likes a drink at a weekend was an alcoholic too. They'd tell me I was in denial; that I really was an alcoholic. But I didn't have bottles hidden away in nooks and crannies. I didn't crave alcohol. I went out and got pissed every now and again but never in my life had I woken up and thought, 'I need a drink. Now!'

This basic disconnect with what the people at Sporting Chance were trying to achieve meant that every morning I'd sit in a meeting with a counsellor for an hour just saying what I thought he wanted to hear. A decade later I'd do the same with the psychologist I had to see before I went into the *Big Brother* house. Each contestant was supposed to be in with him for two hours. I was in there five minutes – 'No problem, Razor, you'll be all right.' I suppose that shows just how good I was at covering up the real me. Or not buying into the process. In every AA meeting, just one thought dominated my mind: 'This isn't me.' And I still believe that now.

I was totally detached from the whole experience, like I was watching myself getting through the days. I couldn't wait to get finished and go home. Couldn't wait to bin the 7 a.m. yoga sessions and the workouts in the gym. 'Why the fuck am I in a gym?' I'd think. 'I've been stuck in gyms half my life. How is this supposed to be helping me?' I never bought into any of it. The low point came during a group session where a therapist tried to put us at ease by revealing his own foibles. First up, he told us he'd had a wank while thinking about his wife's sister. I was just getting over that when he asked, 'Anyone here ever fucked a chicken?' A very embarrassed silence was only made worse when he answered his own question: 'I have, out of my mum's freezer.' Really it should have been us giving him counselling.

I want to make it clear that I'm not having a go at Sporting Chance here. While it might not be top of my list of dream holiday destinations, it does some truly great work. And by letting me see I wasn't alone in being someone in and around sport who had lost their way, I definitely felt a lot more normal than I had in a long time. There were loads of familiar faces from the sporting world, among them a prominent TV presenter and a Premier League striker. Footballers, rugby players, cricketers – over the next few weeks I'd watch them bawling their eyes out, opening up to all kinds of addictions and problems.

I get that, from the outside, where people work hard and every penny counts for something, sportspeople throwing thousands upon thousands away on booze, drugs and gambling just looks like people with too much money behaving like twats. But you have to look at it more realistically. As a footballer, for instance, you end up spending a lot of time on your own. After training in the morning, players are always told to go home, put their feet up and sleep. Even now, I can sleep in the afternoon and still go to bed no problem at 10 o'clock at night. That amount of free time often means footballers, especially single footballers, are more likely than most to get heavily into something like gambling. They're back home every day at half past one with nothing to do and money burning a hole in their pocket. It's not like they've got a family to look after or a partner to go out somewhere with. Even if they recognise that they're gambling too much, that it's got a grip on them, they wouldn't think of going to Gamblers Anonymous, same as a boozer wouldn't contact Alcoholics Anonymous. Those places are for people lying in the street, aren't they? And that's where organisations like Sporting Chance can step in and bring some reality to the situation; to make them see that they have a problem the same as absolutely anyone else.

Footballers will, I'm sure, continue to find themselves addicted to gambling, alcohol, drugs, or whatever. It's true, money and young blokes isn't always a good combination. But I'd ask that we're not always so quick to judge. Thing is, as a footballer you only have to make a couple of bad decisions at a young age and you're branded for life. A bloke who spends his days losing thousands on the Stock Exchange, on the other hand – thousands of other people's money, by the way – he's normal. He wears a suit and so that makes it all OK. It's always the footballer who makes the front pages.

Whatever the circumstances of their addiction, without intervention I've seen people spiral horribly out of control. I've watched the misery of that scenario in action and the lengths to which people will go to hide it. When I was at West Ham, John Hartson had a big problem with gambling but had worked out ways to make it look like he had things under control. If other people were around, he'd ring the bookies – this was the days before gambling apps – with a thirty-quid bet. What those people didn't realise was that John had told the bookie beforehand to stick another nought on the end. A £30 bet was actually for £300, and so on. When he won, he'd stick the nought back on the end. Do that and it looks like you've got this gambling game worked out. They say the one person you can't kid is yourself but I do actually think John came to believe his own trick – and you soon start losing a lot of money like that.

John didn't fool me. I could see how gambling had got under his skin like a disease. John's natural personality was like mine, the life and soul of the party. But when his money went down the drain, that version of John disappeared with it. There were times when I'd look at him in the dressing room and he'd somehow be there and not there at the same time. I'd speak to him and it wouldn't even register. It was like he'd been taken over. Invasion of the brain-snatchers. Thankfully, in the end, John confided in me what he was doing and I'd sit with him when I could to make sure he wasn't tempted to pick up the phone. Ultimately, by taking responsibility for what was going on, he cleaned himself up. Pity the same couldn't be said for the bookies who were happy to be a part of that extra nought scheme which allowed him to fool his friends, family and himself for so long. These days John won't go near anything that even remotely resembles gambling. I've done dinners with him and he won't even buy a raffle ticket. I'd never even thought of that, but he's right – every time you buy a ticket you're having a punt.

To be fair, 90 per cent of single lads can deal with having free time. It's the other 10 per cent that's the problem. And, had I not married young, I'd have been in that 10 per cent for sure. I wouldn't have liked those long afternoons on my own. Self-discipline was never my strong point. I'd definitely have gone off the rails early doors. Let's face it, I was bad enough as it was. What kept me on at least a kind of straight path with money was that I had responsibilities. Yes, I earned good wages, but with them came a bigger mortgage, better cars, clothes, holidays, schools. No way was I ever going to splurge a load of cash up the wall on the horses every afternoon. If I'd not had that responsibility, who knows? For me, gambling was a *Sliding Doors* moment. It only ever really affected me once, when me and a few of the West Ham boys had a few bottles of wine round Piccadilly one afternoon and ended up playing a game of Spoof – basically you have to guess how many coins everyone has got in their hands and the loser pays a forfeit. Usually that forfeit's something like buying a round. On this occasion it was to go straight to the nearest Jaguar showroom and buy a top-of-the-range car with (get this!) the winners choosing the colour and the trim. And guess who lost? I could only watch as they had the best time ever telling the bemused salesman my requirements – bright purple on the outside, beige on the inside, with lime green trim. I was nearly sick on the floor just thinking about it. And that was before I'd signed the cheque. But that was just footballers being daft, it was nothing to do with gambling as an addiction.

Thankfully, I went in a different direction, although one that harmed me and those around me, nonetheless. I was addicted to drink, not through a desperation for alcohol, but because it was fuel for another addiction – Razor. Like John Hartson and hundreds of other footballers I've definitely got an addictive personality, it's just my addiction was slightly more unusual than most. Now I'm older and wiser, with a lot of harsh lessons learned along the way, I'm not addicted to anything. Sporting Chance played its part in that journey because seeing others in such dire straits gave a huge amount of context to my life. But I was still travelling a long road, and in all honesty, at that point in time, Sporting Chance's message – that if I stopped drinking my life would improve – felt like a load of bollocks. I packed up the booze, like they said, and felt totally miserable. If my marriage had been hanging on by a thread when I came out of the jungle, now that thread finally snapped. It was a hellish period. Perhaps I should have drunk more. At least then I wouldn't remember it.

After six months without a drink, I went out and got pissed. I was bored with not drinking. I missed the social side, having a laugh, sharing stories. Going out and nursing a Coke all night wasn't me. I didn't want to go out if it was going to be like that. When you mix in drinking circles, when your mates are all getting pissed and seemingly enjoying it, it's not easy to be the one sat there with a soft drink. I've heard a few non-drinkers say the same – it's like suddenly you have to explain yourself, to clarify what it is that's suddenly made you boring and no fun anymore, although to be fair to other people, chances are they're not actually thinking that. You just think they are.

When Sporting Chance found out I was drinking again, I was invited back for a refresher course. Second time round, I didn't drink for a year and a half. Again, though, in the end I felt I was missing out on a side of life that I enjoyed. I'm the sort of person who thrives off company. I like having fun, being around people who make me laugh, and sometimes having a drink is part of that. The problem for me in the aftermath of retirement wasn't alcohol, it was the directionless mess my life had become. I was lost without the camaraderie of the dressing room and so alcohol was a crutch to get me through each twenty-four hours. I wasn't an alcoholic but I was using drink to replicate what had gone. Going out on the piss day after day was a very easy way of not facing up to the fact that the life I once had was never coming back. I'd told myself the pub was the answer to the void in my existence and I believed it. I couldn't bring myself to recognise that getting pissed with random blokes in various boozers was actually nothing like the dressing room, where laughter and friendship, good times and bad, come from a shared sense of purpose; from travelling every rise and dip in the road together and experiencing each other's ups and down along the way.

While I'd convinced myself that going down the pub to enjoy the craic was the way to bring some meaning and happiness into my life, the reality was I only made the pain worse for myself and those around me. The real tragedy is that in the end I lost touch with my two children with my first wife. After the inevitable break-up, the divorce was prolonged, with disputes about payments lasting years. I would always send Josh and Millie birthday and Christmas cards but would never hear anything. It was a torture, and one which, as ever, I kept to myself. I wouldn't tell anyone what was going on in the background. When people asked how I was, the answer was always the same – 'I'm fine.' And if people asked how Millie and Josh were, I'd say they were fine too, as if nothing had happened. I didn't want to put my burden on other people, for them to feel embarrassed for asking. And anyway, the way I looked at it was that mates would have their own problems; the last thing they'd want would be to hear about mine. My way forward was based on blind hope. I just wanted the whole sorry episode to be water under the bridge and for us all to get on with our lives.

These days, I still drink, but I don't go missing. Gradually I've come to understand my relationship with alcohol. While I wasn't an alcoholic, I was definitely dependent on it socially. It allowed me, or so I thought, to fill the gap left by football, of being able to share the daily ups and downs with others.

If I was sitting at home feeling terrible, what was the alternative? It made sense to get out and meet people rather than wallow on my own. In my head, drinking delivered. In my head, it was keeping me going. I know people will read this and think, 'Not an alcoholic? Who's he kidding?' But genuinely these days I can take it or leave it. Yes, I know that's what they all say. But I can go out for a meal and just have one glass of wine or some water. The toxic element of alcohol was the reliance on it to be Razor. I could see no end to my problems. The only solution in my head was getting drunk and being him. Coming to terms with that issue has pushed alcohol into the background in my life.

What you come to realise over time is that a buzz can be a buzz whether alcohol is involved or not. I get a big lift now from standing up in front of audiences and making them laugh by telling stories from my career. I don't need a drink to do that, and I don't see anyone expecting me to get leathered before I get to my feet. I've also got a 'Get Out of Jail' card. If things are getting a bit messy, the shots are being lined up on the bar, I can put my hand up and say, 'Sorry, everyone, can't be doing that, I've got a pacemaker.' Beforehand, I'd be walking through an airport knackered at 3 a.m., be spotted by some people in a bar, do a few selfies, and the next thing there'd be a tray of slammers in front of me. At that point I felt almost honour bound to be Razor. How could I let those people down? And then the next tray of slammers would arrive, and the next. No matter how little I wanted to, I always felt like I had to drag Razor out of myself and put him on show. Slowing down on the alcohol isn't always easy when you're well known, you're a 'big personality' and everyone wants to buy you a drink.

Then there was that other great affliction of the drinker: FOMO (fear of missing out). If I didn't go out, I'd worry I'd miss something. Now I look at it differently. I've seen it and done it. I don't need to have the same night out over and over again. I drink in a different way. The FOMO has gone. I do what's right for me. If I want to have a few and have a laugh, fine. If I don't, I don't. If I fancy a drink and it fits in around the family, I'll go and have one. If it doesn't – if I'm picking the kids up from school or whatever – then I won't. It's as simple as that.

I don't drink much now because I don't want to – because I feel good about myself. I don't want to go backwards. I've had that life of being out drinking all the time and I don't want to be that person anymore. Because it's horrible. People always look back on a night out like it was the best thing that ever happened. But what they don't remember is the aftermath: the feeling like shit, the pissing people off around them, the wasting of entire days. If Razor Ruddock wants to go out and get drunk, I'll put the kibosh on it, I'll stay at home. If Neil Ruddock wants to go out, then that's fine. More than happy to have a couple of glasses of wine with that bloke. He's a cuddly old bear. Not a grizzly bear, a cuddly bear. If there's anyone who'd rather see Razor in the pub, tough. He's not there anymore. But Neil's there, and you're welcome to come and say hello to him instead.

8

SO WHO WAS RAZOR?

Everyone still calls me Razor. The only person who calls me Neil is my mum. And judges. Even my missus calls me Raze.

I was christened by my Tottenham teammates when they made the link with Donovan 'Razor' Ruddock, the Canadian heavyweight boxer. Before that, at Southampton, the fans dubbed me Schuster, after Bernd Schuster, the German midfielder. It wasn't to do with looks – Schuster was known as the Blond Angel – it was more to do with the fact we both could deliver a free-kick like an Exocet missile. Even my goal celebration earned a title at Southampton. I don't remember it too clearly, but after scoring a penalty in a relegation six-pointer against Newcastle, I celebrated by jumping up and down so hard that I inadvertently invented the Ruddock Stomp. It's moves like this that convince me they really do need to invite me on to the next series of *Strictly*.

Razor was a name given to me, so was me as seen through other people's eyes, not necessarily my own. Nicknames are funny like that. Once you've been given one, that's it. It's there to be lived up to. After all, if you met someone called 'Mad Eddie' and he turned out to be the most mild-mannered bloke in the world, you'd be pretty disappointed. Similarly, if you're called Razor, people might well expect you to be a little bit unpredictable or dangerous. It's not a nickname you'd imagine is attached to many librarians, for example. 'What's that, madam? The new Harry Potter? You'll need to go and see Razor on the front desk.' A surgeon might get away with it but even then it sounds a bit bloodthirsty. 'Hi, I'm Razor. I'll be taking your appendix out today.' For a boxer, on the other hand, Razor's a great nickname. It sends out a message – mess with me and you'll regret it – I'm sharp and I'm deadly. Handle with care. But I was a footballer, not a boxer.

To be fair, in the beginning, Razor felt a natural fit, a natural extension of my personality. In truth, I liked it. It indicated a pretty full-on kind of character. I never needed much persuasion to be the centre of attention, and Razor – big, boozy, loud Razor, carrying everyone along with him – was the ideal guise for such escapades. Roy Evans called me the Pied Piper because everyone would follow me. They knew there'd be some madness along the way. Of course, what I then discovered is you can't be the Pied Piper one day and not the next. There's no escape. Once you're it, you're it. What happens when the elation of a big night out ebbs away? Being the Pied Piper doesn't work when you're on your own, when all you've got to call upon is yourself. In those moments, I'd feel empty and low. Then, back in the dressing room the next day, I'd have to stoke Razor's furnace all over again.

Football seems to have these big presences more than any other sport. Look, every manager wants that 'up' character – the one who turns up at the training ground on Monday morning, when heads might be down after a bad result, with a big 'All right, lads! How we doing?' The one who can start something off, get people laughing, blast away those negative thoughts and bad memories, lift his colleagues up off the floor. Yes, football is about ability, but it's about so much more than that. In a changing room, raising the mood is important. Managers wanted me for what I could bring to a team off the pitch as well as on it. They're not stupid, they do their homework on that kind of thing. I lost count of the number of times a manager said to me, 'Come on, Razor, get the lads going today! Let's see them having a laugh.' If players are moping around, a manager is never going to get the best out of them. If I could snap them out of it, then I was happy to make that happen, not least because I was improving my own mood as well. When I was driving to training on Monday morning thinking, 'Bloody hell, I had a nightmare on Saturday, I really don't want to do this', by flicking on the positivity afterburners I was lifting myself along with everyone else. Again, being Razor seemed to work, but equally it was a short-term fix to a long-term problem. While Razor could lift other people's spirits, he could throw mine into a black hole.

When Razor entered my life looking like the perfect fit, I hadn't considered how restrictive his cloak would become. How often I'd want to throw it off and just be me. Sometimes I'd pull into a lay-by on my way home, sink down in my seat so no-one could see me and read the paper for half an hour, listen to the radio, have a few sweets, just to give myself a rest from being him. I was always glad of the chance to be a different person to the one I portrayed in the dressing room or on the pitch; glad of the chance to escape from the football environment full-stop. One time, when I went on a golfing trip with my brothers and a few old mates, we were sitting in a minibus and 'True' by Spandau Ballet came on the radio. Every one of us joined in. It felt great because these were people I went way back with. People who just knew me as me. Later, when we went out in the town, and people saw me and expected me to be a certain way, out came Razor again. There have been literally hundreds of times in my life when I've got back to my hotel room, shut the door and breathed a sigh of relief. With Razor switched off, I'd sit on the bed taking in the quiet and staring into thin air.

People don't always appreciate what a high-pressure job being a top-flight footballer is. Or they think the money makes the pressure go away. After all, real pressure is not being able to put food on the table or pay the bills. As a working-class lad, I get that – even if my mum did buy me a steak before a game – same as I get that playing sport for a living makes you one of the luckiest people on Earth. But that doesn't mean there's no pressure, especially playing for a club like Liverpool where the spotlight is as constant as the demand for success. I went there as the most expensive defender in the world. And there's an expectation that comes with that, multiplied by a thousand at a club which is a place for legends and heroes. I get how Harry Maguire must have felt going to Manchester United.

When you walk into a football club with a price tag on your head, the pressure doesn't come from the dressing room. Those people are footballers the same as you. None of them are making a big deal about it. It's the papers and the TV, the fans having a chat in the pub, social media too these days, that build the wave of expectation which follows you around. Those bits of downtime where you're switched off from the madness become really precious. It's nice to have a couple of hours where no-one's trying to talk to you about your job. That's not to say I wasn't always approachable. I appreciate what football and meeting players means to people. Never in my life have I refused an autograph or, more recently, turned to someone asking for a selfie and said, 'Fuck off!' But at the same time if you're desperate for that bit of headspace, constant attention can become tiresome. I don't mean that in a bad way, I'm just being honest. Whoever we are, we all have times when we just want to be left alone. I understand why a lot of sportspeople get into fishing for that very reason – standing in the middle of a river you're a lot less likely to have your mental break interrupted than you are at a bowling alley, the cinema, or wandering round a shopping centre.

I did actually try the old rod and line once but it didn't quite work out. I caught this massive pike and the sight of it scared the life out of me. I had to get a mate to get it off the hook! That was the end of fishing for me. Golf was better and is still my go-to escape now because concentrating sucks everything else out of my head. Compare that to what I found at the end of my first season at Liverpool when I took the family to Disney World in Orlando. One day we headed to a massive Adidas shop. As I walked round the corner, there was me, in my Liverpool Adidas kit, on a huge poster hanging all the way down over the front of the store. That's when it hit me: 'Fuck me, I'm famous!' This was America. They didn't even really like football. And there I was, about fifty feet tall. Frightening. More likely to make customers run in the opposite direction than buy something. But it told me something – going to Liverpool had made me a superstar. And if I had to be fifty feet tall then Razor was the one who was going to help me do it.

Razor, though, was becoming not an extension of my personality but something that covered it up. In the big macho world of football where showing emotion was seen as a weakness and the best blokes were the loudest blokes, the ones with the biggest, funniest stories and a constant glass in their hand, he gave me a massive shield to hide behind. Every feeling, every mood, Razor was the answer. Nothing was off limits. A great time was had by all, or so it seemed. Truth was, at the end of the night, all too often Razor was left head-in-hands in that hotel room. How did I deal with that? Go out and be Razor again of course.

Over time I came to understand that repeating the cycle wasn't really addressing the problem, but as a footballer I was blind to it. At Crystal Palace, I actually had 'RAZOR' on the back of my shirt. By then a lot of overseas players sported their nicknames or first names. Jimmy Floyd Hasselbaink had done it at Leeds, as had Jordi Cruyff at Man United, and so I asked the Palace kitman to do the same for me. I'd have carried on doing it too, had the FA not fined me £75. I appealed that punishment at a tribunal and actually only lost on a technicality. If I'd been down as Razor Ruddock on the team sheet handed to the officials before kick-off, I'd have been all right. I should have remembered that rule from Liverpool, where I had the number 25 shirt in recognition of that £2.5 million fee. I actually had a dot put in the middle so I was 'RUDDOCK 2.5'. Again, fined.

Incidentally, playing for Liverpool in Europe once I was given a shirt with 'RUDOCK' on the back – only one D. I had to go and see the referee before kick-off, who then had to go and see the UEFA officials. It was a nightmare. I only had the one top and they had to 100 per cent verify who I was before I took the field. It was like they were identifying a body. They stopped just short of asking for dental records. At least I wasn't fined, for once.

Being a different person to the one you let everyone see is a pretty big secret to keep. It's also incredibly damaging. The longer you do it, the more trapped you become, until eventually you can see no way out. As a footballer especially there was definitely no light at the end of the tunnel. I played in an era when to be anything other than a 'bloke's bloke' was to leave yourself open to ridicule and abuse. Even if you did want to talk to someone about your inner thoughts and feelings there was no-one to go to. Football clubs were old school, run by tradition. There was no desire to kick that old-fashioned male stereotype into row Z.

If there'd been a door at Anfield with 'Sports Psychologist' written on it, would I have gone and knocked on it? Maybe. Maybe not. I don't know. In all honesty, probably not, because if you were a professional sportsperson back then, talking could be seen as a sign of weakness. Imagine if word got out. It wasn't just what your teammates might think, it was the opposition team, and especially their fans. Once fans think you've got a weakness, they're all over you. It's a hard enough game as it is without that going on as well. It was obvious that any player who was suspected of struggling mentally would be shipped out. In fact, make that any player who just didn't fit the assumed pattern of what a footballer should be. I never knew anyone who was gay in football, but I've been in dressing rooms alongside hundreds of different players so that person must have been there.

The only gay player to come out in my time was Justin Fashanu, who sadly went on to take his own life. My belief is that, in the eighties and nineties, had a manager known a player was gay, they'd have moved them on. Again, more than anything, because of the crowd reaction. Things, hopefully, have changed but back then a gay player would have received a massive amount of abuse. It would have been a ninety-minute barrage and a manager would have seen that as a distraction his team didn't need. Clearly that's wrong but I'm convinced that's how it would have been. To come out as gay would have been incredibly tough. Football was seen as a man's game and that was that. The media played its part in keeping that stereotype alive. Why, after all, when I went on *Celebrity Wife Swap*, was I, a footballer, placed with Pete Burns, a flamboyant popstar, if it wasn't to create a 'when worlds collide' kind of scenario? I think they thought it would show me up as a bit of a dinosaur when in fact me and Pete got on like a house on fire. I've always liked turning that macho footballer image on its head.

Whatever your dressing-room 'secret', speak up and you were playing Russian roulette with your career. Although, like I say, this is all hypothetical – the speaking-up option simply wasn't there anyway. These days there'd be a plan of action. People at the club would have your back. Back then, I reckon if you said you had depression the first reaction of most people would be, 'Christ! I hope it ain't catching!' At the very least you'd be thought of as weird. Just look at the players who were different in some way. Graeme Le Saux was thought of as odd because he read a broadsheet newspaper. Pat Nevin stuck out because he was his own man and would quite happily go off and see a band play in the middle of nowhere than have a big night out with the lads.

At Liverpool, we had Nigel Clough. Not only did Nigel not drink but on an away trip he used to do his brother's company accounts. The only numbers we were looking at were on a pack of cards. Nigel was a lovely bloke, very funny. He would mix and have a laugh, but doing accounts on the team bus? That was something else. Now I can see he was just doing something that worked for him. Maybe it took his mind off the game to come. The rest of us? 'Weirdo!' It showed a lot of strength on his part to do that in front of his teammates and not be bothered about being singled out. At least Nigel was the same as us in that he liked crosswords. Except he'd do *The Times* cryptic and we'd do the *Daily Star* quickie. We'd take it in turns to do an answer and if we couldn't get it, we'd have to put a tenner in the pot. The rest of the lads never realised there was a phoneline you could ring for the answers. I'd sit there with one earphone in and win every week – I just couldn't solve the puzzle that was myself.

The fact that puzzle got more and more complex wasn't just about not seeing a psychiatrist. A professional set-up at the training ground, with all the amazing facilities they have now – physios, nutritionists, dieticians, chefs – would have made a massive difference. Yes, these people make you feel good, play good, but more than that they're someone to talk to. Suddenly you've got an environment where help is available at every turn.

If you want people to be open about themselves, give them somewhere which encourages it, which screams out loud that you care about their wellbeing. Every business should have that person in place to say, 'Are you OK?' A happier person will always perform better whatever they do, whoever they are. If counsellors had been embedded in a club alongside those other helping professions, and if what they could do had been explained to us, then maybe we would have used them after all. People will say that's nonsense, that we'd have been too set in our ways, but I know it's true because I've heard people say it. I had a game of golf recently – footballers versus rugby players – and afterwards we got talking about whether we'd have been better players with the help of counsellors and dieticians. My answer to that was, 'Forget being a better player, I'd have been a better person.' And that's the thing, whatever's going on in your head is about something much bigger than sport. With that help, and the encouragement to use it, we'd have looked after ourselves better, which would have been better for our brains, our bodies, for everything.

I've heard countless players of my generation say how much they wished there'd been a door to knock on. As it was, there was nothing. And if there isn't anything, that makes you think the only thing to do is keep your thoughts to yourself. A club would do something about it if you had an injured leg, but your mind? Nothing. Forget it. Keep it to yourself. Hope it will change. When you have a mental health issue, your brain is injured. The only solution we knew was to self-medicate down the pub with alcohol until the pain went away. When I started at Liverpool, they never even had a physio let alone a psychologist. Now they've got a throwing coach for Christ's sake! These were multi-million-pound globally-recognised clubs being run like part-time businesses. There'll be clubs now in the National League with better set-ups, for brain and body, than pro-clubs back then.

As I mentioned in the beginning of this book, the one person I met who really got what I was living through wasn't a footballer but a popstar. Robbie Williams used to hang around with the Liverpool boys a bit in his Take That days, whether he liked it or not. One time a few of us were heading off to Marbella for a few days and we gave him a call to see if we could drag him along. Unfortunately, he had a recording session with the group. Personally, I felt this was a bit of a cop-out. OK, singing was his job, and being in Take That was kind of what he was all about, but I wasn't going to take no for an answer. 'Right, let's kidnap him.' We rolled up at his house unannounced, grabbed him and his passport and chucked him on the minibus. Next thing he knew he was on the Costa del Sol, an absence from Take That which I always say helped get him sacked from the group. Actually, thinking about it, if that hadn't happened he'd never have gone solo and we'd live in a world without one of the greatest songs ever, 'Angels'. It's all down to me. I really am amazing, aren't I?

Being around Robbie was great. In Marbella one day he turned up in a full Port Vale kit – socks, the lot – with a leather football under his arm. All he wanted to do was play football. All we wanted to do was karaoke! But what I remember more than anything was what he said about living a public life as one person when in private you're entirely another. The danger of one version of yourself smothering the other. We were, after all, both in industries where moping around – or looking like you're moping around when in fact you're just really struggling – was never going to play well with our audience. The answer was always to push those feelings to one side, put the face on and get out there. Robbie's words, 'Don't end up like me', were probably the most important anyone ever said to me. They stuck with me down the years, helped me focus and lifted me out of a lot of negative thoughts.

We went our separate ways for a long time – there's only so many times you can kidnap someone without them getting wise to it – but then Robbie got in touch with me again after *Harry's Heroes*. He'd been through the whole lifestyle change thing – got himself off drink and drugs – and found a settled life with a wife and family. He wanted me to go over there and spend a few days with him to help sort me out. That's a lovely thing for anyone to do and something for which I'm very grateful. I'm not saying me and Robbie are the same, we're not. He's bipolar – his mood is up, down, up, down. I can kind of relate to that, except I think I'm generally happier. I can get myself out of bad times, see a clear road ahead, whereas Robbie seems to go from month to month. But what I do know is we've both had desperate times behind closed doors. We've both inhabited worlds nobody saw but us.

To escape that world, I'd stick my Razor mask on and head for the nearest crowd of people, the nearest bar, in search of oblivion. Glad to report I'm different now. I love being on my own. I eat on my own quite often. When I'm away doing after-dinner speaking I'll often walk into a restaurant and happily sit there, not pretending to read a book or to look at my phone or anything. It doesn't bother me when I see other people looking uncomfortable about it. I'm just enjoying the peace and quiet and that's all there is to it. I don't know why we've made it such a big deal that people should want to do stuff alone. Sometimes it's the complete mental recharge we need. But instead we stick labels on people – loner, anti-social, miserable – and make them feel bad for wanting to do something that's actually really good for them. I'll stick my Razor face on when I get up on stage to make sure everyone's entertained. Until then, I'll be me. Same as when I get back in the car I'll relax, and relax even more when finally I sit down back at home. At that point, Razor's done his job for the night. I don't need him anymore. I can have a laugh in my own time without him. Being a little more strict with Razor's on/off switch is something I should have learned a lot earlier. But, like they say, experience is wasted on older people, and I'm the perfect example of it.

The only time Razor has come back big time recently was when I was in a taxi with my agent Ben's daughter. One second we were singing ABBA songs, the next BANG! – an horrific smash with another car. Massive impact. Glass everywhere. Blood, the lot. My reaction was to go into full-on frenetic Razor mode, getting her out of there and making sure she was all right. Razor, in that moment, was useful. He was the man to be, because he had that crazy energy – for once in his life put to good use. It was a bit like being the Incredible Hulk. Something happened to transform me into this other version of myself. Except the Incredible Hulk never woke up in Kent the next day with a broken rib.

It makes me laugh how in so many places there's the true me and the created me. Take my Wikipedia entry. It's full of things I've never done while half the things I have done aren't in there. I told Rob about my version of why he was sacked from Take That and he actually said if I stuck it on my Wiki-pedia page, he'd go on there and verify it! I keep meaning to do it because it would add so much to the complete and utter bollocks that's already been written about me.

Pre-Wikipedia, there were people determined to create Razor-related bollocks that was a bit more public. I had the tabloids on my back for years, being accused of all sorts of escapades – birds and booze mainly. One time at Liverpool I was in a pub near where I lived in Formby when I got a tip-off from a mate who was a paparazzi photographer. 'Watch out, Razor,' he told me, 'there's two birds coming down to the pub. There's a tabloid trying to stitch you up.' He knew precisely what was happening because he was the one who'd been asked to take the photos when they sat next to me to make it look like I was being a naughty boy. I appreciated that call – by the time the snapper arrived, I was gone.

Of course, there were plenty of real-life escapades I was mixed up in over the years, but those days are long gone. I'm not as mad as I used to be, but I get I'll always be Razor to most people, and I'm happy with them calling me that. I've had people bellowing 'Razor!' at me for years – blokes trying to shake my hand while I'm stood at the urinal – and it ain't going to stop now. I'm like a magnet. If I'm in a restaurant full of celebrities and someone walks in off the street, you can bet your life they'll ignore everyone else and come straight over to me – 'Razor!' – because they see me as approachable, which I am. So long as no-one tries to nick my naan bread, I'm fine. By the way, I'm the exact opposite. If ever I see someone famous when I'm out and about I never go over – I'm too worried they won't know who the hell I am! I couldn't deal with the embarrassment.

There is one thing you'd think being called Razor would have brought me. To this day I've never been sponsored by a razor company. Ian Wright's there shaving his face in front of the nation and I've had nothing. Winds me up. Razor manufacturers, I don't care what bit of me I have to shave – beard, back or bikini line – give me a call. But while I'm not quite as clean-shaven as I might be, I definitely do still get recognised. I had one person come up to me in London the other day: 'Did you used to be Razor Ruddock?' I had a think about it afterwards. I suppose I did used to be Razor Ruddock. Not so much anymore.

9

HARD GUY? ME?

I do sometimes wonder if just being Neil Ruddock, without the Razor, might have changed other people's expectations and perceptions of me. Maybe it would have made it easier just to be myself. Let's face it, life would have been a lot different if I'd have been called Cuddles. Then again, does Cuddles really work for a central defender? Especially considering some of the brick shithouse strikers that were around in my day. It definitely wouldn't have put the fear of God into Duncan Ferguson, that's for sure. There were times when it was useful to have a reputation.

I never got into any scraps or punch-ups away from football. It was just on the pitch that I was horrible. Or 'committed' as I'd put it. It was the 'Craig Short incident', as it's come to be known, that cemented my reputation. That headbutt was my ultimate red mist moment. To be fair, the Notts County centre-back had just trodden on my

Southampton teammate Alan Shearer. If it hadn't been Shearer I'd never have reacted. He was my little mate. He couldn't even drive at that point. I used to pick him up, take him home. He was my lapdog. I'd have kept him in a handbag if I could. When someone stamped on him, I was never going to run the length of the pitch and shake that person's hand. And I wasn't the only one to feel like that. By the time I arrived from my cross-country run there was a ten-man brawl going on. I just provided the finale. An admittedly abrupt one which left Short needing four stitches above the eye. Maybe it wouldn't have been so bad had I not tried to run away from the scene of the crime only to bump straight into the ref. It was like being at school – the crowd parting after a scrap and there's the headteacher stood there: 'Ruddock! My office! Now!'

I bump into Craig now (not physically) and we get on fine. Actually, I look at him and wonder what the bloody hell I was thinking, putting one on him. He was a big tough central defender and wasn't afraid of putting it about himself. But it wasn't him that annoyed me, it was what he'd done. The ultimate irony of course was that he went to play at Blackburn, with Shearer. And I wasn't a million miles away from joining the pair of them.

It happens in football – someone you consider your biggest enemy ends up becoming one of your best mates. Ian Wright, for example, was never anything less than a grade one pain in the arse. He used to come up to me during a game: 'Oi! Razor! Your wife makes a lovely breakfast!' That wasn't so bad, par for the course. What I really hated was him scratching me, on the neck, the back of the arm, anywhere, when no-one was looking. It would sting like mad because of the sweat. Instinctively, I'd swing round to see what was happening and he'd be straight on at the ref: 'Look, man! Look at this lunatic! He's trying to hit me!'

'But he just scratched me!'

'I never touched him, ref! He's a lunatic, I tell you. A lunatic!'

Of course, I had a few tricks of my own. I made sure I hurt Wrighty a few times. By that I don't mean outrageous fouls. If a striker was pissing me off, my favourite trick was to 'accidentally' tread on their big toe. Fourteen stone coming down through a metal stud tended to shut people up. Other players you could put off their game by going at them verbally. Paolo Di Canio had a fuse shorter than a bookie's pencil. As a defender you'd light the blue touchpaper and watch him go. Most infamously, Paolo shoved referee Paul Alcock to the ground during a game between Sheffield Wednesday and Arsenal after being sent off for an altercation with Martin Keown during a classic twenty-man brawl, a moment of madness which cost him an eleven-match ban and a ten grand fine, even if Alcock did, as they say, go down in instalments. A few days later at West Ham, me and Wrighty caused our own little furore by mimicking the incident. Wrighty scored, ran to the side of the pitch, I gave him a shove and he staggered backwards to the floor, returning to his feet only to deliver me an invisible red card. The FA, as ever, didn't see the funny side. We were called before them and fined. Of course, West Ham only then went and signed Paolo. I'll be straight, me and Wrighty were seriously worried what sort of greeting we'd get after our little piss-take. Paolo, though, was a gent. 'You two – crazy!' he told us, and left it at that. Phew! We could remove the body armour from under our shirts.

It was Eric Cantona I most looked forward to winding up. Any bloke who answers a perfectly reasonable question in a press conference by banging on about seagulls, trawlers and sardines has got to be fairly highly strung and I enjoyed playing on that element of his character every chance I got. Some people might think the easiest way to get under Eric's skin would be to kick him a few times, but then again maybe those people have never stood next to him. The bloke's six-foot-two and built like a buffalo. No, I preferred the subtler approach, by which I mean I irritated the shit out of him by continually going up behind him and turning his collar down. Why nobody had done it before, I don't know. If it was such a big deal to him to wear it up, it was clearly going to piss him off royally if someone kept reversing it.

The game I chose to do it in already had a massive edge. Not just Man United v Liverpool, which is tasty enough, but Eric's first game back after his nine-month ban for his kung-fu kick on that idiot at Selhurst Park who'd given him a mouthful of abuse. I'll be honest, when Eric launched himself at that 'fan' that night, there were more than a few of his fellow pros who thought it was a job well done. Initially, I couldn't believe it when I saw it on telly. But then you think, how much shit are people meant to take? The more I saw it, the more I thought, 'Good for you, mate!' He'd only done what every other player has wanted to do at some point or other. Not that I was shaking his hand when we ran out onto the pitch at Old Trafford. And he certainly wasn't shaking mine when I took the chance, as Peter Schmeichel took a goal-kick and we were stood next to each other, to start messing with his questionable fashion sense. Straight off, he took a swipe at me and from that point on, I knew I'd got him. If a player's concentrating on you and not the game then he's not doing his job. I did it again and he retaliated a few seconds later with a high tackle that got him booked. He was risking a red by sticking his elbows out every time I got near him, served with a side dish of verbals.

Eric's English wasn't great but he'd clearly mastered the phrase 'fat bastard', not to mention the international sign language for 'big belly'. I was laughing my head off – until I also heard him say the words 'in the tunnel'. It occurred to me then that whatever he couldn't get away with on the pitch he was planning on doing ten times as bad at the end of the match. As I say, Eric was a big bloke. His actions at Crystal Palace also suggested if he wanted to lay one on somebody he'd do it and sod the consequences. When the ref blew up, Eric made for the tunnel. I made for David James. The Liverpool goalie was six-foot-four. His physique was Greek statue meets hod carrier. If ever you need an Atlas ball moving, give him a bell.

Waiting in the tunnel, the second I appeared Eric started giving it large. I don't know what English teacher he'd been using in Manchester, but they'd certainly done a lot of work on the word 'fuck'. If that included 'Fuck me, the size of him!'

he didn't say it, but the sight of Jamesy definitely seemed to dampen his desire for violence. I'd pretty much forgotten about the whole thing when we entered the players' bar for a post-match drink. And then I felt a tap on the shoulder. I knew exactly who it was. I was just wondering how far to the nearest hospital when Eric tapped again. I turned round. Eric smiled and handed me a pint of lager. What a bloke! Sadly, our paths never crossed again. Who knows if I'd have wound him up all over again? I do know that, along with Bergkamp and Zola, he was the best footballer I ever played against.

A good defender notices when an opponent is getting wound up – and then does their level best to wind them up even more. The hope is that eventually they snap and do something completely mad that ends up with them being sent off. When I was at West Ham, Arsenal's Patrick Vieira was the perfect example. Paolo Di Canio had already riled Vieira by firing West Ham two goals in front, the Frenchman's mood not improved any by him constantly being outplayed by Marc-Vivien Foé in midfield. I felt it wouldn't hurt to remind Patrick every now and again that Marc-Vivien was making him look a complete muppet, and I was delighted to see Patrick wasn't taking my words particularly well. He didn't say anything back, but he didn't need to – his feelings were clear from the veins sticking out the side of his head. He'd already got himself one yellow card when he then decided to boot Paolo up in the air. 'Ah! My work is done.' Being a considerate sort of person, I headed to the scene of the crime to bid Patrick farewell. He wasn't terrifically pleased to see me and let me know with a face-full of spit. It was absolutely disgusting – spitting at someone is the biggest no-no in the game – and my first reaction was to want to be sick. My nausea eased off a few days later when the FA handed him a £45,000 fine.

With some clubs the hardest bloke wasn't always on the pitch – or at least wasn't meant to be. Sir Alex Ferguson once came running on after I'd given Mark Hughes a bit of a tap at Old Trafford. He was waving his arms and shouting something in Glaswegian. I wasn't having that. 'Look, Taggart,' I told him, 'fuck off!' I could see a few of the United lads trying not to piss themselves.

It was a piece of advice I never gave to Fergie's namesake and fellow Scot, Duncan Ferguson. Big Duncan wasn't known as 'Dunc and Disorderly' for nothing. Over the course of his career he was handed nine red cards, plus the small matter of a three-month prison sentence for an on-field assault. Had he been starting out now he'd have been diverted to the MMA circuit. Dunc fed off abuse. Give him a mouthful and it was only going to make him try twice as hard. 'Ignore him!' was what everyone said, and after seeing him in the flesh in the tunnel before a game at Everton I couldn't help feeling it was very good advice. He looked like something out of a comic: Angerman. Only once did I put those words of advice to one side, after he went in hard on the Liverpool defender, Robbie Jones. I was so angry with the tackle that I spent the rest of the game kicking Dunc from one half to the other. But that was the only exception I ever made. Dunc was not a man to rile, as those two lads found out when they robbed his house. I've often wondered how stupid you'd have to be to break into Big Dunc's house. One of those blokes found out when Dunc laid into him so badly that he actually had to resuscitate him before the cops came.

I had some sympathy with the Everton man. My house was also broken into while I was on Merseyside. The first I knew something was wrong was when I heard an announcement over the Anfield PA: 'Will Mrs Ruddock please come to reception?' That's definitely not normal. Immediately I was thinking, 'What the fuck?!' Turned out two blokes had got into my house – without realising I had two massive Dobermans, a breed which is OK with letting people into places, but very much against letting them back out. When the police arrived, there was blood everywhere. The intruders had managed to lock themselves in the ensuite and the dogs were waiting for round two outside. They were proper guard dogs. Hard dogs. Unlike the ones we'd had as a family in Ashford. When Dad came back from Saudi Arabia we had a big celebration. We were all kipping in the house, on sofas, the floor, all over the shop, and somehow none of us noticed until we woke up that we'd been burgled. The villains must have bribed those hounds with steak, or maybe my brothers' Spam. Actually, that makes the robbers sound cleverer than they were. Among the stuff they took was a load of Saudi currency. The coppers alerted the local banks and the minute someone appeared with a load of Saudi riyals, they nicked 'em.

Burglar-mashing or not, compared to Billy Whitehurst, Big Dunc was a puppy dog. Plying his trade mainly out of the top flight, Billy might not exactly have been a household name, but Jesus he was tough. Scary tough. At Southampton one time, we were playing Sheffield United. I was pleased to see Billy wasn't playing and I was having a much easier ride against the Blades' Brian Deane. I was just walking off at half-time when I saw something hurtling towards me, like that big round rock in *Raiders of the Lost Ark*. Shit! Whitehurst! Before I could react, he got hold of my shirt and ripped it wide open. I wouldn't have minded – well, I would – but in those days spare shirts weren't a thing. I had to go out in the second half with my shorts under my armpits to keep the bastard thing in place.

The striker I used to really relish coming up against was big John Fashanu, aka 'Fash the Bash'. The thought of getting stuck in with Fash, elbows flying, bones crunching, no quarter given, really got me going. It was the little quick ones I didn't like, the Pat Nevins of this world, buzzing around all over the place like horrible little wasps. I might have had a bit of trepidation going into a game against those sorts of players, but with the big lads it was fair game, a level playing field.

Fash's Wimbledon colleague Vinnie Jones is the hardman I'm asked about more than any other. And yes, we did used to kick lumps out of each other on a regular basis, although so similar were we that we might as well have just kicked lumps out of ourselves. Me versus Vinnie was the clash of the social secretaries. Being the big character around our clubs, we'd both become the person everyone else looked to for enter-tainment. Vinnie was also, like me, a very different person on the inside. Beneath that outer shell, he is a lovely man and it was an awful tragedy when he lost the love of his life, Tanya, to cancer. Vinnie – big macho Vinnie, star of *Lock, Stock and*

Two Smoking Barrels – is a great example of a man, who many would think the epitome of the alpha male, opening up emotionally. I think half the nation cried with him when he spoke about his loss on *Good Morning Britain*, and he's become a really strong voice in the fight to persuade men to talk about their feelings. Vinnie was always a lot more sensitive, a lot more intelligent, than people realised. We'd be on the bus to an away game and he'd be pointing out all the birds he could see out the window, telling us stuff about kestrels and the like that none of the rest of us would ever have known about. He was great company but not necessarily in the way that people might imagine.

Being at Wimbledon suited Vinnie's on-pitch image. Plough Lane was a bastard of a place to visit whatever club you played for. As if a team full of hardcases wasn't bad enough, they'd turn the heating off in the away dressing room and soak the floor. You can imagine on a cold winter's day what it was like in there. When I was with Spurs, I'd stand with wet feet in the freezing cold thinking of the underfloor heating we had back at White Hart Lane. Wimbledon always had a few tricks up their sleeves. If they were playing a passing team like Spurs, the grass would be left about six inches long so the visitors couldn't move the ball around properly.

Then they'd tip a bag of sugar in the tea urn for the half-time cuppa. Second half, you'd have an attack of the shits.

If Vinnie was one of the leading UK experts in removing skin from bones, then not far behind him was Stuart Pearce, aka 'Psycho'. That's a bloody great name to be fair. Proper old school. Not that his reputation bothered me. At Southampton early in my career, I absolutely destroyed Stuart and split his eye open. I smashed him up in the air and he jack-knifed and hit his head on the floor. He jumped up and gave me a real stare – one that said vengeance was just around the corner. 'Shit!' I thought, 'I've proper had it now!' I had visions of seeing out the rest of the season from a hospital bed. Luckily, I had backup. Behind me were Terry Hurlock and Jimmy Case, the latter being the hardest footballer I ever played alongside. Jimmy had won every trophy going with Liverpool before moving on to the Saints, which is where I encountered a man who wasn't just a great footballer but an absolute assassin. Most of us have a little bit of iron in our blood. Jimmy was iron with a little bit of blood. I was delighted only ever to play on the same side as him, which included my first game as a visitor to Anfield. Jimmy was my captain.

'From corners,' I asked him, 'is it one hand up for the near post and two hands up for the far post?'

He looked at me. 'Let's just get a corner first.'

For sure, a couple of slightly more refined defenders than Case and Hurlock on my side and I'd have been for it against Pearce. To this day, Stuart won't let it go. Last time I saw him, he whacked me in the ribs.

'Eh, what was that for?'

'That tackle!', he said, and walked off.

I'll be honest, I loved that sort of confrontation. One where it was either me or the other bloke. I wasn't a bully – I wasn't that horrible – but if there was a 50/50 tackle to be had, I wasn't going to shirk my part in it. In the case of the Pearce clash, neither of us touched the ball. We'd seen each other coming and knew from five yards out that whoever went for the ball would be in massive trouble. Get the ball and you're 100 per cent going to get hurt because you're in no position to shield yourself. Go for the tackle and you've got a chance. Stuart was one of my heroes, but when it came down to it, if someone was going to get kicked I'd rather it was him than me.

There was a lot to admire in Stuart. 'Psycho' he might have been on the pitch, but again, like Vinnie, he was lovely off it. Good job really. Being Razor is one thing, being Psycho is a bit different. I was named after a boxer. Say 'Psycho' to most people and they think of the knife-wielding killer from the Alfred Hitchcock movie. The other difference between me and Stuart was that he was incredibly confident in being his own man. He barely drank and away from football his big passion was punk rock. He quietly got on with his life in his own way.

Once you've got a reputation as a hardman it tends to follow you around. Barely had I made Liverpool my long-term footballing home when I broke ex-Anfield favourite Peter Beardsley's cheekbone in a testimonial for Ronnie Whelan, a game which also doubled as my debut. Like I say, I never arrived anywhere quietly! Peter, playing for his hometown club Newcastle, claimed it was a deliberate act to confirm my 'hardness' to the Anfield fans. It wasn't, it was just an accident. After all, crunching a club legend is hardly a great way to announce yourself to a new set of fans. It was all a bit ugly between myself and Peter at the time but we're mates again now. He actually messaged me to congratulate me on my weight loss.

While I'll admit I did revel a bit in the hardman image, the tag has sometimes been a burden down the years. When you're asked constantly to talk about the most destructive tackles of your career, you do sometimes find yourself thinking, 'You do know I could play a bit as well?' Liverpool didn't pay £2.5 million for someone to go round kicking people up in the air. In my entire 426-game career I was sent off eight times, which, for a proper in-the-thick-of-it defender I don't actually think is too bad. There's sixty yellow cards in there as well, but again that was what I was there to do. My job wasn't to let people take a Sunday afternoon stroll past me and calmly stick the ball in the net, it was to let them know that to get what they wanted they were going to have run through a brick wall. Run through any brick wall and it will occasionally leave a scratch.

Were an alien to read this book they might get the impression that football is a game played by violent, plodding, ruthless thugs and of course that's not true. A small minority of players do actually have speed, agility and skill. Their job is to avoid the violent, plodding, ruthless thugs and either score or create goals. I mention this because my first room-mate at Spurs was none other than the great Osvaldo Ardiles. Seventeen years old, barely out of the Millwall youth team, I was waking up at 3 a.m. and five feet away in the next bed was a global footballing icon. This man, snoring away, occasionally muttering incomprehensibly in Spanish and doing sleep keepie-uppies under the continental quilt, had kissed the World Cup in 1978, the first World Cup I can remember, and one of the best, with its showers of tickertape and that great theme tune on the BBC. Lying in that bed was part of that incredible team – Passarella, Kempes, Luque. It was a shame Ossie couldn't reel off the names of the 1985 Millwall Third Division runners-up – Cusack, Lovell, Chatterton, Stevens – but I forgave him because I loved that World Cup and I wanted to know everything, Ossie happily chatting away to me, and me pretending I was understanding.

Ossie was brilliant. Considering everything he'd achieved in the game he had no arrogance at all. Before my Spurs debut – still a teenager, remember – I was sitting there in the dressing room feeling more than a little nervous when the diminutive maestro piped up.

'Razor,' he said, in that distinctive South American twang, 'when you get the ball at the back and you cannot give it to me, the best player in the world, or Glenn Hoddle, the second best player in the world, do you know what to do at this precise moment?'

'Er, no,' I replied.

He looked at me. 'Fucking panic!'

By making me laugh he took all my nerves away and that was Ossie all over. He wanted people to be happy. When he went to Fort Lauderdale Strikers, he invited me to go over to Florida and stay with him in the holidays. That's what happens with roommates, you develop a special relationship with them. Ossie looked after me and I'm still great mates with him now. I call him 'you little Argentinean c***'. People overhear me and say, 'You can't do that, he's Ossie Ardiles.' And I say, 'Yes, I can. He's my roommate.' And anyway, he's not averse to giving a bit back. The night England lost to Croatia in the semi-finals of the 2018 World Cup, me and Ossie did an event at a big hotel in London. We were both pissed and at the end of the night it was down to me to get Ossie in a cab and back home. It was a right palaver. No sooner had I bundled him in than he was climbing back out the door. 'No, no, no!' he kept shouting. He then started unbuttoning his shirt. I wondered what the hell he was doing. Even for Ossie this was remarkable behaviour. Eventually, after a bit of a struggle, he pulled something out. It was hanging round his neck. His World Cup winners medal! He'd had it on all night. He flashed it at me, got in the cab and fucked off.

Me and Ossie love each other. I expect it's like being in the Army where you've got your bunkmate or whatever – these things are there for life. Although looking back now, he did treat me like his butler. I'd have to run his baths for him while he sat having a smoke. In fact, while I'm writing this, I'm just starting to wonder if that was why he wanted me as his roommate. As the youngest in the team, I was bound to do whatever he asked. Oh, who cares? To be Osvaldo Ardiles' butler, what a privilege! And I did make the set-up work for me as well. One of the first things that struck me about Ossie was how lovely he smelled. His aftershave was clearly out of my league. I was on Brut and Blue Stratos whereas he had these proper aromas about him. Rich. Exotic. And so when he was out the room – occasionally he'd go down to the hotel lobby to have a fag and look suave – I'd nick a bit. But he was always wise to it. If you're going to nick someone's aftershave always wait until they've used it first. I was 100 per cent in awe of Ossie, but he never expected me to be like that. Early on, for instance, he taught me how to sing 'La Bamba'. Not long after, he came along and sang it at my engagement party. What a man.

Some players sit halfway between the hardman and the physically unimposing type of character. They're more of a scamp and this is the category the aforementioned Alan Shearer falls into. Me and Alan were ushers at each other's weddings, while, as I'm always telling people, he's godfather to my children and I'm father to his (jokes like this illustrate why I'm a very good after-dinner speaker – the best in my price range). But any footballer will tell you that when you're playing against a mate there's only two things you want to do: beat him and hurt him. Which is perhaps why when he was at Blackburn and I was at Liverpool he ended up pretty much trying to throttle me on the pitch. I'd trodden on him one too many times for his liking and in that moment the fact that we were best mates and lived a hundred yards away from each other in Formby counted for nothing. To be fair to Alan, I'd already had one go at permanently wrecking those toes of his. At Southampton, a few of us raided his hotel mini-bar when he was in the bath. He jumped out to chase us and we dropped the bottles. They smashed and he ran over the glass in bare feet. Two of his toes were hanging on by the skin. It almost ended his career before it had begun. It was actually one of the few moments when I really stopped and looked at how mad and potentially dangerous – to myself and others – my behaviour could be. 'This ain't funny,' I told myself. 'I have to stop.' But course I never did.

Toes aside, Al's a great example of how hard it is to hurt great players. Right from a young age they've been kicked and so they develop ways to stop it happening. Look at Gazza and how good he was at putting an arm out to hold people off.

Other players see a tackle coming a mile away. They know how to avoid it. It's what makes football great – you don't have to be built in any particular way to play it, you just have to avoid making contact with the likes of me.

Being big, little, hard, skilful or whatever means nothing when the conditions make pretty much every footballing attribute irrelevant. Take Tottenham's fourth-round FA Cup tie at third-tier Port Vale in January 1988. Spurs legend Jimmy Greaves reckoned that his old team's biggest problem would be finding the ground, but he hadn't factored in a pitch that was 90 per cent mud, not particularly helped by the fact that the home side got the fire brigade in to water it in the run-up. We were 2–0 down to a team 18th in the old Third Division by the time I headed one back – my first senior goal for the club – but it was too little too late. The whole experience was horrible. Snow in the air, freezing cold. I couldn't wait to get on the bus and get out of there. I'm still picking bits of Vale Park out from under my toenails nearly forty years on.

In reality, you can never predict what's going to leave you in a heap on a football pitch. There are just too many variations. Take the ball. These days it's the same for every game. Back then, clubs could pick and choose. If you were playing away on the Saturday, during the week you'd use the opposition's ball in training to get a feel for it. The worst was the Mitre Ultimax, used by, among other clubs, Manchester United. That ball always felt heavy. Get whacked with it and you'd have Mitre stamped on your leg for a week. Get it full in the bollocks and hopefully you weren't wanting any more children anyway. Even then, with your testicles now situated somewhere between your liver and spleen, the pain didn't compare to the ball that flicked the back of your leg. Sounds daft, but that's the worst of the lot. Thankfully, at Liverpool we used the Adidas Tango, something else which made me know instinctively that this was the club for me. The Adidas Tango was the very ball that had been used at that 1978 World Cup I'd so loved. Quick in the air, it was perfect for a bit of South American flair. It flew off the foot and was kind on the testes.

Of course, the people with the ultimate power to hurt, indulge, or look after you in football aren't players at all. Managers are the ones you really have to worry about. They're unpredictable, fiery, stressed, and occasionally violent. That's why you've never seen David Attenborough try to film one. Sitting in a nest of gorillas is one thing, sitting between Alex Ferguson and Graeme Souness something else entirely. When dealing with this particular breed, occasionally it really is best to keep your distance.

10

MANAGING RAZOR

I was lucky. The majority of the managers I played under were great people. They taught me a lot about the game and even more about life – and that applies to Terry Venables more than anyone else. Terry might not have had the success in England of some other big-name club managers, but of all the bosses I ever worked with he was the best. Why? Because he understood players as people as well as footballers.

Terry took an interest that went way beyond just trying to get the best out of me as a sportsman. And he was totally genuine. In the players' bar with my mum and dad after a game, not only would he come over and say hello to them, but he'd know both their names: 'Hello Joyce, hello Ted.' He'd go across to another player's family and I'd hear him do the same. He did that because he knew a happy player is a better player, but he also did it because he knew it was right. Fifteen years after Terry left Spurs, my dad was at Stansted Airport when he felt a tap on his shoulder: 'Hello Ted.' It was Terry. Fifteen years and he hadn't forgotten.

I loved Terry, simple as that. He knew how to get the best out of individuals. He realised that 'happy' doesn't necessarily mean letting players off the leash. It means understanding what they need. That might mean an arm round the shoulder but equally it might mean a kick up the backside. He could be hard on me, but he did it only because he knew me inside out, what made me tick. If I was having a bad game, he'd look at me at half-time: 'Your dad's come here? And you've played like that?' He knew how that would sting, and how badly I'd want to put it right. Make no mistake, Terry was a very clever man. If he was overly nice to me, he knew I'd relax too much. If he said I was letting my dad down, wasting his time, he knew I'd bust a gut to change that. It's all about recognising character and motivation.

No-one could match Terry for knowing how to talk to players. He'd have one-on-ones all the time. He'd ring me up the day after a game to talk it through – what I could have done differently, or what I should do to improve. He realised that talking to me straight after a bad game wasn't always a good idea. I knew if I'd played like a twat and didn't need to analyse it the minute we got back in the dressing room. It was too raw and Terry knew that. Sleep on it and then go over it was a much better idea.

That level of understanding made life easy for players. You only have to look at what Tony Adams says about Terry – the best coach he's ever worked for. And that includes Arsene Wenger and George Graham. He was also the only boss who instinctively knew how to manage Gazza. Terry used to compare him to a big fish – reel him in and let him go again, reel him in and let him go again – and he was absolutely right. Like every other player, Gazza adored Terry and responded to him. Look at that Euro 96 squad and the players who were in it – big characters, big names, all sorts of personalities. And Terry got the best out of all of them. They knew they could trust him completely, a lesson that, weirdly, I learned when as a young player he sold me back to Millwall. Terry's predecessor David Pleat didn't seem overly enamoured with the purchase he'd inherited from Peter Shreeves, especially when on a pre-season trip to Sweden me and the rest of the boys ignored the club curfew and headed off into town to find a nightclub and enjoy a few beers. As the new kid on the block I was the gopher, back and forth to the bar getting drinks for everyone – basically, an alcohol-infused version of cleaning people's boots. All was going smoothly until I turned round, several bottles of Pils in hand, to be faced with Pleat. I'd never had him down as a disco dancer, and from the look on his face, and lack of medallion, I thought it unlikely he'd decided to start now. With the Gibb brothers harmonising in the background, he made it clear that he saw my future in the game as being limited. Glitterball spinning overhead, he told me I was better suited to being a security guard than a footballer – just the boost you need when forging your way at a new club.

As it was, Pleat's future at Spurs would be more limited than my own. He was sacked not long after and Terry came in, showing his belief in me by handing me a starting debut at White Hart Lane against, of all sides, Liverpool. Their defender Gary Gillespie welcomed me to this sparkling new world by fracturing my ankle – although I never realised it at the time and played on to the end of the match. That's how hard I was. It was a week later when an X-ray finally showed up the damage. After recovery and a handful more games, Terry had a word. 'Go out and learn your game,' he told me. 'I'll sell you young and buy you back.' My initial thought was, 'Yeah, right. Of course you will.' But then he'd ring me every three months: 'You had a great game yesterday, well done,' or

'Have a think about doing it this way next time.' So he was still giving me advice even though he wasn't my manager. He didn't want me to think I'd disappeared off his radar. He genuinely wanted me to develop, not just as a player but as a person as well. And of course he stuck to his word. One day at Southampton – where I'd moved from Millwall – I got a message. It was from Terry: 'Right, you're ready now. I want you back.' Sheer managerial brilliance.

Compare that to how the Craig Short headbutt situation was handled at The Dell. Next day, I was in a restaurant and the manager, Ian Branfoot, tracked me down and rang me.

'We're putting you on the transfer list,' he told me.

'Was that your decision or the club?' I asked.

'My decision,' he replied.

Two months later I was back in the team, going great guns, and Ian wanted me to sign a new contract.

'Sorry,' I told him. 'You said you didn't want me.'

'No, no,' he said, 'that was the club.'

'No,' I reminded him. 'It was you.'

Soon after I was back at Tottenham with Terry and a year later I was signing a contract at Anfield. Some might say I ended up playing for two of the biggest clubs in the world because I nutted someone. That's not really true. Like I say,

Terry was keeping an eye on my progress. But Ian Branfoot's overreaction meant I was on my way out of Southampton anyway. When a player steps out of line, you deal with it and move on. So long as they keep doing their job then it's soon in the past. I had my moment of madness, was punished, and that should have been the end of it. Transfer listing me was totally over the top. To be fair to Branfoot though, I'm sure that he was getting leaned on from above to take the 'proper' action to ensure that Southampton's reputation as a family club remained intact.

It's a funny thing being a footballer. Yes, you're a sports-person, but you're a financial asset as well. You're there to be bought and sold, moved from here to there. Talk is cheap in football, so to have someone like Terry who said he'd buy me back – and then did – meant a lot. He was very astute in doing that. He let me get the games under my belt, waited for me to get better – still keeping an eye on me all the time – and in return landed himself a proper good defender. Terry understood the player he'd got, uncompromising but skilful with a great left foot – the 'tin-opener' as Ian Wright once called it when later I scored for Liverpool against Arsenal. Terry felt a lot of refs didn't get a player like me, and instead just followed the line that my game was about hurting the opposition. When I was harshly sent off by Philip Don against Crystal Palace, Terry confronted him in the tunnel.

'Mr Don,' he enquired, 'if I call you a c***, would I be in trouble?'

'You would, Mr Venables.'

'OK,' pondered Terry, 'what if I thought you were a c***? Would I be in trouble then?'

'You wouldn't.'

'Well then,' he paused, 'I think you're a c***.'

And then after just one year it all came crashing down. Terry's light touch was at complete odds with club chairman Alan Sugar's authoritarian style. The pair fell out and Terry was sacked. To say I was devastated would be the biggest understatement of all time. I felt so comfortable at Spurs, had just got a new house, the kids were settled at school, and then suddenly it had all been thrown up in the air. It was a huge down in the dumps moment. Something truly great was going on at Tottenham and then in a flash it was taken away.

Along with being dropped for the FA Cup Final in 1996, Terry Venables leaving Spurs is the other big 'if' moment in my life. I can say for sure that if he'd stayed at Spurs I'd never have left. That team he was building around the likes of Teddy Sheringham, Nick Barmby, Darren Anderton and

Sol Campbell would definitely have gone on to challenge for the title. Terry was absolutely different class. He would have made it happen. I know also that Terry wouldn't have left me. If he'd got another club job straightaway, he'd have taken me with him. I'm confident in that because I know how much he loved me. I was his captain and we both desperately wanted success. Even when it all went wrong at Spurs and we both went our separate ways, Terry still kept in touch. As I say, he valued people for who they were, not just as footballers.

With Terry gone, that left me to deal with Sugar. When Terry had signed me again, he'd recognised I'd had the odd disciplinary issue at Southampton but told me he'd double my wages after a year. I had a good first season – only sent off once, which wasn't bad for me in those days – was made the captain and became a fans' favourite. Terry had been all set to make good on his promise before being sacked. Sugar, who went on to become sacker-in-chief on *The Apprentice*, turned his back on Terry's deal. 'I don't care what Venables said,' he told me, 'it's not happening.' He tried to fob me off with a hundred quid a week more but I refused. Sugar's response was to put me on the transfer list. When he saw the calibre of the teams who were coming in for me he realised the player I was, backtracked, and tried to get me to sign a deal. It was like Southampton all over again – sorry, mate, too late now. I left Spurs because of Alan Sugar, simple as that. A shame, because after Terry, my pal Ossie Ardiles became the manager. 'Don't worry about Razor,' he promised Sugar, 'I will get him to sign.' By then of course, I was already halfway out the door.

'Sorry, Ossie,' I laughed. 'I ain't signing anything! I'm off!'

'But Razor . . .'

'No, mate. Apologies, but you'll have to find someone else to run your bath.'

There was no shortage of interest in my signature. Kenny Dalglish at Blackburn, Graeme Souness at Liverpool, Kevin Keegan at Newcastle, Glenn Hoddle at Chelsea, Brian Clough at Nottingham Forest, Walter Smith at Rangers – the list went on and on. I promised I'd speak to everybody. I met Kenny at Blackburn on the Monday and then the day after I headed across to Anfield. Graeme met me at reception. He gave me a quick guided tour – 'there's the boot room' – and before I knew it we were heading down the steps onto the pitch. 'Touch that!' he said. I looked up. He was pointing at the famous 'THIS IS ANFIELD' sign. I didn't need asking twice. I'd seen so many Liverpool legends reach up as they went out on to the turf. It sent a shiver down my spine. Silently, we walked out into the middle of the pitch, surrounded by massive stands. The atmosphere of the place was amazing, like it was alive. 'Can you imagine playing here?' he asked. 'Give me the pen,' I replied. And that was it. Liverpool wanting me meant I went from down in the dumps at leaving Spurs to total unrestrained excitement. Anfield, the history, Keegan! – and now I was going to be a part of it. I couldn't wait to hit the motorway and get started.

I went to Liverpool because there was nowhere better to play football, to improve, and be part of something so, so huge. I'd been to Anfield as the away side and it was hard. You were up against not just a great team, but the tradition, the crowd. So the opportunity to be on the home side, to hear the Kop sing your name, was just incredible. OK, Blackburn went on to win the league, but I didn't care. I knew I'd made the right decision. In a roundabout way, it's another thing to thank Terry for – if he hadn't stood up for himself at Spurs, and incurred the wrath of Alan Sugar, I wouldn't have played for what was to me the best team in the world.

There's only really one other English football manager of recent times who's looked on with the same affection as Terry, and that's Bobby Robson. Not many people realise I played under Bobby but back in the eighties the full England manager would take charge of age-group teams, wanting to see the players of the future coming through. Going away with England was my first time in the hands of a different kind of manager. Until then, first with George Graham at Millwall, and then with David Pleat at Spurs, I'd been playing for gaffers who were a bit sergeant major. Everything was very regimented with the younger players. Bobby, on the other hand, was more like an uncle – approachable, nicer, asking about you and your family. He had to be like that to some degree, because otherwise how else was he going to get to know you? Your club manager knew everything, whether you needed an arm round the shoulder or a kick up the arse. The England boss knew nothing.

I learned early on that, as with Terry later, Bobby was a man who understood what made players tick, what they needed to hear. On a trip to South America with the Under-19s, I was sent off twice in three appearances. In Uruguay, a geezer hit me off the ball and then dived on the floor to make it look like it was me up to no good. In Brazil, I got a straight red for a tackle that would have got no more than a wag of the finger off a ref over here. I came from a world where getting sent off once was pretty much guaranteed a managerial bollocking. Getting sent off twice would be a ducking stool in the team bath. That was for your club. Getting your marching orders while representing your country could surely only be a hundred times worse. But Bobby couldn't have acted faster to put those fears aside. 'That's football,' he told me. 'You've got to learn quick where you can and can't make tackles like that.' That's how Bobby saw these trips, as an education – for us to see how differently the game is played around the world. To him, they were a vital part of the learning curve if a player was ever going to perform well at international level. For Bobby it was a big deal taking age-group teams to different cultures. By the time I was 19, I'd played in South America and China. I'd stood on the Great Wall. No-one had done that. Well, they had, just maybe not from Ashford in Kent.

Most people would expect a few young lads on a dream trip to the fleshpots of South America to be out there causing all sorts of mayhem, but actually we were very well behaved. When we went to Rio we were specifically told, 'Don't leave the hotel!' because the crime rate was so massive. Although I did wonder how bad it could be. I mean, try going down the Old Kent Road on a Saturday night. When we were allowed out it was to a place of real nightmares – well, for someone scared of heights. I had to get off the cable car up to Sugarloaf

Mountain at the halfway point and wait five hours for every-one else to come back down.

Regardless of the risk of getting shot or plummeting from cable cars, South America was also an official trip and so it was drilled into us that we were representing our country abroad and we had to look and act the part. Ambassadors don't particularly like to be greeted by half-pissed surly youths with their trousers hanging round their arse.

Admittedly, by the time I was with the Under-21s in Toulon in the south of France, standards of behaviour had slipped a little. We were all hoping to sneak out at night. The FA were clever though: they put us on an island off the coast. Well, it worked at Alcatraz. Although at Alcatraz there wasn't the chance to play strip poker with the hotel waitresses in your room.

Like Bobby and Terry, Harry Redknapp was another who knew the value of players feeling wanted, of them feeling part of a group. We had a great mix of young and old at West Ham and we had a lot of fun together, not least with our signature tune, 'Country Roads' by John Denver. When the referee's bell sounded – the signal it was time to go out – Harry would shout, 'OK, put it on!' We'd be into that song all guns blazing.

Standing on the benches, banging on the roof, ceiling tiles going through. Now 'Country Roads' is hardly known for raising the fires of hell in listeners, but that song just worked. Instead of sitting there all nervous with five minutes to kick-off, we were shouting and bawling: 'Fucking come on!' 'Let's have it!' We played Man United once. 'What a dressing room that is,' Terry Sheringham, then at Old Trafford, said to me afterwards. And he was right. We had amazing spirit and headed out onto the pitch smiling and happy with adrenalin in our veins while the Man United boys were all sheepishly sat there with a stoney-faced Fergie. Harry got that dynamic – another reason why he was a bloody good manager. He'd walk out before the madness started, but he knew full well what was going on. At Coventry once, they actually turned the electricity off in the away dressing room so we couldn't do it. They hadn't remembered that power also comes from batteries, and trying to stop us just made us even worse.

Having a great atmosphere among a group of players counts for a lot. If you've got a team who love being with each other you'll get an extra 5 per cent of performance from every one of them. Add that up and that's a good few extra points at the end of a season. Don't believe me? There's been some great examples of clubs who've had brilliant players but haven't translated that into success. Chelsea in recent seasons is one of them, and lack of team spirit at Stamford Bridge has been mentioned again and again. Harry definitely knew how to keep a group together. Even if you were on the bench he made sure you felt part of the plan. Before the match he'd say, 'Don't matter whether we're winning, losing, or drawing, after sixty minutes you're coming on.' That meant instead of being pissed off to have been left out of the starting eleven, you sat there for an hour absolutely raring to go. When the time came, you'd be out there like a rat out a trap. At a time when legs were tiring, suddenly there was someone on the field going at 110 per cent and everyone fed off that. That's why Harry would have been a great England manager: he knew how to get the best out of a group of blokes. People say he didn't have the technical knowhow, but you're talking about the best players in the country. They don't need coaching. That's not what managing at international level is about, it's about building a unit. Same goes for the amount of bollocks talked about tactics. When you haven't got the ball, you need to keep your shape; when you have got it, the best players will do their thing. If you think a great player is picking up the ball in midfield and thinking back to what the manager said in the team meeting forty-eight hours ago, you must be mad. Messi? Do you think he was thinking about tactics when he was sticking them in for fun? Managers can over-think the game. Look at all the teams these days who insist on passing out from the back. And look at how many times even the best ones get caught out making six or seven passes either inside or on the edge of their box. Harry let players do what they were good at, he didn't force them to be something they weren't.

If Harry did have a problem, it was that he hated people not taking him seriously. If he was giving a player a bollock-ing and someone else burst out laughing – and by someone I mean Ian Wright, who would always be pissing himself behind Harry's back – he'd shout, 'Oh fuck off!' and stomp away. But equally Harry never held grudges. He'd say what he felt needed saying and then two minutes later everything would be back to normal. Some managers would let a falling-out rumble on for a couple of days, create a really bad atmos-phere, but not Harry. 'It's gone.' That's what he'd say. Again, clever man-management. Things move fast in sport. It's the future that matters. Dwell in the past and you're done. The other problem Harry had was that he didn't always engage the filter between brain and mouth when speaking. One time we reached the FA Cup quarter-finals. 'West Ham have got to win the FA Cup this year,' he told us, 'because that'll mean I'll get lots of money and can buy some better players.' As pep talks go, it was certainly different.

Harry's loved, in and out of football, because he's a down-to-earth, normal bloke, the only manager I know who has tomato sauce on spaghetti bolognaise, although my dad did used to have Daddies brown sauce on his roast dinner. Harry's one of those blokes who's always got a twinkle in his eye, a daft comment on his lips. The problem is that some might say the same about me. And so what happens when two people like that meet head-on? Me and Harry found out when West Ham saw fit to fine me twenty grand after a small brawl with my teammate Mike Newell while playing golf at Gleneagles. I say 'small brawl' as it was just a bit of pushing and shoving. A big brawl would have involved something eyewatering with a sand wedge. Since this wasn't the case, I felt twenty grand was a bit on the harsh side and so not only did I appeal but I flew in a world-renowned brief from South Africa for the FA tribunal. The bloke was just as good as I hoped – forget Judge Judy and all that lot – and barely had proceedings started than he'd trampled the case against me into the ground. The club would have to pay me back the cash. Punching the air, I turned to Harry: 'Unlucky, H!'

Of course, these top barristers don't come cheap. While I was celebrating, the lawyer promptly slapped in his bill to the tribunal – £30,000. In a court of law, this was the done thing. Except this wasn't a court of law. The costs weren't covered by the FA. They were, it was explained, covered by the person who'd engaged him – me. I'd gained twenty grand and lost thirty. It was Harry's turn to look at me: 'Unlucky, Raze!'

Considering the affection between me and Harry I'm sure there must have been people in that room who thought, 'Remind me, just why are these two up against each other?' But actually it was the club who fined me, not Harry. And my attitude was always to take it as far as I possibly could. If I feel someone or something's trying to get one over on me, that's what I'll do.

I'm pretty sure no-one ever got one over on Graeme Souness, at least not without the bruise to prove it. Graeme was my sort of manager, strong and determined, and my sort of footballer, no-nonsense but could play as well. I knew from experience that crossing him wasn't a good idea. In my early days I'd played in a 'friendly' against Rangers at White Hart Lane. I went in hard on their striker Iain Ferguson and was just taking a breath when a snarling Souness, player-manager of the Glasgow club at the time, took hold of me by the neck and thundered what felt like the entire history of swearing into my face. I actually reminded him of the incident when I signed for Liverpool. I was 18 at the time of that White Hart Lane clash and enquired if he'd still do the same to the somewhat larger player in front of him now. He assured me he would and we left it at that. Soon enough I saw his combative side was indeed still very much alive. He used to make me laugh in five-a-sides. I was convinced he'd come up with a plan to bypass the awkwardness of dropping players – he'd just go in hard and put them out of action for a few days. You could guarantee you'd be playing on Saturday if he picked you on his side. Playing for the opposition, look out!

When Graeme resigned as Liverpool boss I was rocked back on my heels. That familiar feeling of being down in the dumps but not really knowing what to do about it. As a footballer, it's never good to see the manager who signed you walk out the door, but it was more than that. I loved Souness, admired him so much. The club felt different after he'd gone. I'd only been there six months at that point, and he himself had only been there two-and-a-half years, hardly a chance to build something for the future. Maybe the fact he'd turned Rangers around so quickly in his previous job worked against him. Liverpool was a different club, a big beast that was difficult to get hold of and change course. The other major complication was that his old mates were still there. He was trying to manage the same lads he used to go out drinking with. Not easy to play that role when they remember you as 'Champagne Charlie'. His predecessor Kenny Dalglish never had that issue. He was neither a big drinker nor a party animal and so faced a different dynamic when he managed those same big stars.

Graeme's other big problem was that after having massive heart surgery he gave his story to the *Sun*, a paper reviled on Merseyside for the lies it told about Liverpool supporters after the Hillsborough disaster. Once he'd done that he wasn't going to get any second chances to get it right as manager. Believe me, Graeme was cut-up inside that he could have made such an error. He felt he'd let the city down, and still does. I saw him give a speech at a dinner in Liverpool not too long ago and he was in tears about it. The regret he has really is deep and genuine.

For my part, I don't buy the *Sun* and won't do any stories for it. I'm strict on that. When a paparazzi photographer took some pictures of me coming out of a shop with a carrier bag and a folded-up paper under my arm after I'd had the pacemaker fitted, it got printed up in one place as me having just picked up a copy of the *Sun*. I was livid – it was actually the *Star*. My agent had to ring them up and put them straight, which he did, in no uncertain terms.

As the tears confirmed, Souness is a much more emotional character than he ever revealed in the harsh world of professional sport. It makes me wonder if he too was sometimes hiding his true self. When you're one of the toughest footballers ever to play the game it's not like you can let others see you reaching for the Kleenex. And yet he has really opened up in the last few years. I watched him break down in tears on TV, talking about a girl he'd met, who was living with a rare skin disease which meant she spent her days wrapped in bandages. He swam the Channel to help raise a million for the charity that deals with the condition. I thought that was incredible. I had massive respect, not just for that amazing achievement, but for the fact he showed a side of himself that was the complete opposite to that legendary midfield hardman.

An old-school centre-half, Chris Nicholl, my first manager at Southampton, was another hard as nails player turned boss. But Chris was also a thinker, his big skill being the ability to build togetherness in a group. Chris used to take us to army camps, up and down obstacle courses, up and over cargo nets, hauling each other over walls, all the time urging one another on. Then there were the truly epic paintballing battles. You really haven't lived until you've shot Matt Le Tissier up the arse. Not only did we do all that, but it worked. Chris had a lot of young players in that side – me, Tiss, Francis Benali, Jason Dodd – and we'd take on the older guys like Jimmy Case, the Wallace brothers (Danny, Rod and Ray), Russell Osman, John Burridge, Derek Statham. Everyone loved those games. We definitely worked better as a group and that meant better results on the pitch. Chris was 100 per cent ahead of his time. He was doing all this in the late eighties and early nineties before the phrase 'team-building exercise' had even been invented. Within a decade every big corporate business in the country was doing it. But he'd had an angle on how it could work in sport. Magnificent.

Looking back now, I've been lucky to play for managers who, in the majority of cases, saw that players were people, not machines. That might sound daft but there are plenty of bosses who will chuck players out the door the minute the warning signs start flashing. I was gutted when Terry Venables died in 2023, not just because of what he did for me as a football manager, but for what he did for me as a human being. I've heard numerous players say exactly the same about Bobby

Robson. These managers are like great teachers – they stay with you throughout your life. Even more than that, I would say they are father figures. Terry was definitely in that bracket, and so actually, thinking about it now, was George Graham. Regimented he might have been, but equally he knew that, with my dad overseas, I was bound to be struggling. When George gave me my debut in a Freight Rover Trophy match at Southend, he could see I was feeling down – living in digs, missing my family – and he knew playing would give me a massive lift. Like I say, I never realised at the time, but looking back it's obvious. I expect he knew it would also give my mum and dad a boost, knowing I was doing well. George was a clever bloke and a lot more sensitive than he's been given credit for.

I was at the other end of the age scale when Harry Redknapp showed how much he cared. Harry's very much what you see is what you get. And that means he shows his concerned side in a straight-talking way, something which I saw when filming the second series of *Harry's Heroes*. While I'd lost 4 stone before the first series, I'd put it all back on – with interest – tipping the scales at more than 25 stone. Harry was genuinely worried about the weight I was carrying and the lifestyle that had led to me heaping it on. His answer was to get straight to the heart of the matter: 'If you don't change, and quick, you won't see your kids grow up.' He definitely knew how to focus the mind. And of course he was dead right. The doctors backed up his diagnosis 100 per cent.

I always had a lot of respect and appreciation for managers, same as I did for older players. I was quite traditional in that way. I might have had run-ins with authority down the years but those collisions were hardly ever with managers. Even if they had a go at me in front of other players, I didn't take it personally. I never backchatted them or made life difficult in the dressing room. My dad brought me up with that attitude and I believed in it. A lot of the time I knew why they were singling me out – as a shot across the bows of the other players: 'If I'm happy to have a go at a bloke like him, have a think what I might do to you.' And anyway, if I'd pissed them off by staying out late or whatever, I fully expected and deserved to get hammered.

At Liverpool, me and Robbie Fowler got fined for going to Dublin and not getting back in time for Monday morning training. The idea had been to go on Saturday night and come back on the red-eye on Monday morning. When the red-eye was cancelled we knew we were in deep shit. By the time we made it to the training ground – in the afternoon – the rest of the players were long gone. Only Roy Evans and the coaches were still there. 'Your mum's going to kill you,' Roy told Robbie. 'Your wife's going to kill you,' he told me. 'And I'm going to fine you both. Now fuck off.' What Roy left unsaid was that we'd let down him, his coaching staff, the club, the team, the fans and ourselves. He didn't need to say it out loud because his anger and disappointment said it all. And we knew exactly how badly we'd behaved anyway.

When Gérard Houllier came in alongside Roy, he clearly hadn't learned the 'sometimes it's best to say nothing' lesson from his co-manager. He breezed round the dressing room, introducing himself to everyone – until he reached me. 'And you?' he asked, 'what is your name?' I was a bit taken aback. I wasn't expecting him to know my inside leg measurement but I had been at Liverpool five seasons by then.

'Hang on! Have you been in a coma for fifteen years?' I asked him. The rest of the dressing room found it funnier than he did. Barely had Houllier discovered who I was than I was gone. As were the Spice Boys – Redknapp, Fowler, McAteer, and McManaman. Houllier clearly wasn't keen on players who liked going out every now and again. Fair enough, but there's an old saying about throwing the baby out with the bathwater.

My own managerial career was over before it got started. I was on a player's contract at Swindon Town while coaching alongside Roy Evans, whose own time at Liverpool had come to a sad end when sharing the top job with Houllier had – who'd have thought it? – created nothing but a massively confusing mess. Swindon certainly didn't have the financial clout of Liverpool. At best they might have been able to afford Michael Owen's toenails. For me, that meant travelling the country Tuesday and Wednesday nights looking for players that the Robins, then in the third tier, could get for nothing and sell on to keep the club going for a year. There was something else. When you're used to playing at the highest level, the drop in quality is stark. On one occasion I expressed my frustration to Roy. He looked at me. 'If they could play better,' he told me, 'they wouldn't be at Swindon.' You can't really argue with that.

Essentially, at that point I was just waiting to retire, seeing it out until I could claim my pension. What I should have done is spent time away from the game after leaving Crystal Palace and then come back to it. If I'd done that, then maybe I'd have found coaching and management more to my liking. As it was I was worn out by all the to-ing and fro-ing, the constant travelling back and forth to Ashford, and in the end management passed me by. Probably, just as well. I'm really not sure I could have done those post-match interviews without swearing.

'Well, Neil, what do you think went wrong today?'

'*&*!$!&!*&*!&&*!*&$!'

'Thanks, Neil, and now back to the studio . . .'

11

OPENING UP

I'm going to tell you a story. I once shat myself on the M25 driving back from Wales in a Porsche. For a long journey, I usually like to drive in flip-flops and tracky bottoms. On this occasion they were a beige Slazenger pair. At one point I lifted my leg to let out a blast, and that was it – a good pint of chocolate milkshake everywhere. It was in the footwell running through my toes. What could I do? It wasn't like I could walk into the motorway services like that. Instead I pulled in round the back, up against a wall so no-one could see me, had a root around in my golf bag, hoping there'd be something in there I could clean myself up with, found a pair of dirty white socks, which had gone stiff with sweat, broke the ice on a puddle, and cleaned myself up as best I could.

I drove the rest of the way with nothing on my bottom half, my eyes drawn to the petrol gauge, hoping against hope that I had enough to get home. You can hardly fill up with your tackle hanging out, although I'm not sure why, it's hardly a fire hazard. Anyway, that's a debate for another day. Point is, I was driving on fumes and was lucky to make it back in time. Back home, I cleaned up the car – God bless the wet wipe – and thought no more of it. Except, being a Porsche, the car had air-conditioned seats – hundreds of tiny holes for the blast to come through. From then on, every time I switched it on, it was like sitting in a truck-stop toilet. I really do feel for the person who bought it second-hand.

You might wonder why I'd go out of my way to reveal such a horrible tale of woe. And the reason is nothing could better illustrate the kind of thing I was more than happy to tell other people compared to how willing I was to open up about my mental health. I would rather have talked about shitting myself in a car than ever have a discussion about what was going on inside my head.

For a long time, the reality of mental health in my life is I never really thought about it, same as I never really heard about it. Certainly, I never heard mental health mentioned in the dressing room. That's not just me, it's hundreds and hundreds of other players. And out in the real world it's millions and millions of normal blokes.

In the end it was *Harry's Heroes* that changed my outlook. With my physical health on the line I had no choice but to start looking at the way I'd been living my life and the deeper reasons behind letting myself get into such a state. I began opening up on podcasts like *The Men's Room* on talkSPORT, where sports broadcaster Ade Oladipo and YouTuber Rory Jennings talk to guests about mental health, what it is to be a man, all that kind of stuff. It's a podcast I now host myself with Tom Skinner and where I've met some of the most incredible people. Same with *The Ruck*, which is actually a rugby podcast, hosted by former England scrum-half Kyran Bracken – I suppose I qualified because in later years I looked like I might be handy in the front row. It didn't take long for me to feel the overwhelming outpouring of love that came my way from people I'd shared changing rooms with or been mates with for years and years. No-one was telling me I was weak for looking more closely at my mental health, or that I should be ashamed of myself. They were telling me they were proud of me and would do anything they could to help. I had literally dozens of players get in touch. It felt like every day another message popped up: Mark Bright, Carlton Palmer, the list went on and on. The whole experience has been very emotional from that point of view.

Sport is what a lot of blokes talk about and so it's a great way to open up conversations, but like I say, mental health issues don't sit in isolation in the competitive arena. I started thinking about all the blokes who live outside the football bubble – which is pretty much all of them. Are they so different? After all, they're men too, with all the pressure to behave a certain way. Surely they must share the fear of opening up, being seen as somehow weak, and not being a *real* man, whatever that is. And so I branched out into all sorts of areas, including the *All Things Business* podcast with Ben Thomas. Just like with this book I wanted to start a conversation which includes everybody, which leads to something positive happening for people who feel like they want to talk about their mental health but don't know how to go about it. Or are wondering if they should tell their mates. Or what it feels like to stick your head above the parapet. Thing is, I've been there and done that. They can trust me – I know exactly how it feels to be in those positions. I also know you're not mentally weak to admit you have an issue. Mental health issues are an illness. It's a strength to recognise you have a problem and want to do something about it.

One thing I've always known about myself is that for years I was seen as a bit of a geezer. My guess is if there's someone not a lot of people would expect to start banging on about mental health, it's me. After all, it's not long since I was there on *Harry's Heroes*, sitting in a bar in France with a jug of beer in each hand and a bra on my head. You don't generally see people who want to talk about something a bit serious looking like that. When I'd flick through the channels on my hotel room telly at 5 a.m. after getting in from a big night out there was never anyone like that on the Open University. But then again, maybe the fact I'm coming at this issue from a position of peak blokeishness is a good thing. Let's face it, if Razor Ruddock can open up about his deepest, most hidden thoughts, then surely anyone can.

I've always been an emotional person. That came across as passion and determination on the football pitch, but there was a flipside which I never let anyone on the outside see. If I was sat at home on a Sunday night watching *Surprise! Surprise!* with Cilla Black and she reunited someone with their long-lost family, for example, I'd be crying my eyes out. When Kelly Holmes won her double Olympic gold in 2004, I was sobbing in front of the TV. You could see it in her face, everything she had, every fibre of herself, straining to get across the line. I was in a heap, like I'd melted on the carpet.

Same as when I watched *Lassie* as a kid. The things that poor bloody dog went through on its journey home.

But I wasn't going to shout that from the rooftops, was I? Everyone knows blokes don't cry. It's weak to cry. Any situation where a bloke looked like they were getting a bit emotional got the same reaction: 'Man up!' Men have traditionally never asked for help. To admit any kind of struggle, to be down, was a sign of fragility and that was the end of it. 'What sort of bloke goes around asking for help? What's wrong with him? Jesus Christ, pull yourself together.' That's not just in football, it's in life. If we were drowning in the sea, we'd shout for help. Drowning in our own thoughts? 'Get on with it. Pull yourself together, you'll be OK.'

I'll be honest, I've been that bloke who puts undue pressure on someone else. A good mate of mine, who followed my path at Millwall before hitting some real tough times, quit booze for thirteen years – and I spent half that time trying to get him to start again. That's how skewed I was. That's how skewed toxic thinking can be. Someone had done the hard work and there was me in their ear trying to undo it again. I'm sure I'm not the only bloke to do that, and I'm sure he isn't the only bloke to find himself having to resist that sort of pressure, but it's something I'm really not proud of. My only defence is that was the culture we were brought up in. Drink, drink, drink. If you weren't drinking, why not?

By my reckoning, there'll be more than a few blokes reading this who are struggling and would like to be more open about the way they feel. Alternatively, they might be part of a regular group of mates who go to the football, meet down the pub, or whatever, and think someone else among them might be having those kind of issues. You can bet more than anything what's stopping both these types of men from speaking up is the fear of being judged. As blokes we're not supposed to have these kind of conversations. We'll quite happily sit around chatting about all kinds of shit – quite literally in the case of my Porsche incident – so why does opening up feel like such a massive leap? It's because we're not supposed to show emotion. We will, we fear, be laughed at or people will think we're stupid. 'Look at the state of him, what's he going on about? I came out for a laugh, not to listen to him droning on.'

I'll put you straight right now, what you actually find is a whole lot of help, and even more love. Let's face it, as mates, whether you've talked about it much or not, you'll already have been through a lot together. You'll have travelled through a bit of life, seen each other's ups and downs.

All that's changed is that you now actively want to talk about those things rather than hide them away behind the façade of ten pints of beer. I've got a key group of friends who care about me and help me, but I didn't put an ad in a newspaper to find them. They were always there. I just needed to remind myself of that and believe it.

Look at me. I certainly didn't grow up in an environment where we were encouraged to open up. I was a Millwall fan. Like I say, I was on the pitch during the infamous FA Cup riot at Luton Town in 1985. I'll tell you now, on the train home no-one was asking each other, 'Are you OK? How do you feel?' I don't think someone saying, 'Do you know, that's really shaken me up. I might listen to a meditation tape when I get home,' would have gone down particularly well. But you've got to remember there's a very good reason why mental health was never spoken about – for years and years no-one knew what it was. It was a completely different time. It's like going back to 1979 and asking someone what they like to watch on TikTok. Whole generations of blokes grew up and grew old keeping stuff to themselves. In my case, that inability to share my inner thoughts meant I believed I was alone. The only one with problems. Think like that, and before you know it, your brain is dragging you down all kinds of weird dead-ends. The more alone I felt, the more I started to think no-one liked me anymore. The way I saw it, the only part of me that people liked was Razor. Which made it even harder to admit the real me felt terrible. I was Razor, big tough Razor. The minute I admitted I was struggling, I'd burst that balloon. Everyone would see who I really was – someone who, as I saw it, was weak, someone who doubted themselves. I wouldn't have Razor to hide behind anymore.

Then there was the effect opening up in public would have on family, the people who cared about me. I never had a conversation about mental health with Dad. He was from a different generation, and anyway I hadn't started my own mental health journey eleven years ago when he passed away. But as far as my mum's concerned, I'm her little soldier, always have been, always will be. The last thing I wanted to do was worry or frighten her by coming out saying I was in a mess mentally.

A lot of men's unwillingness to talk about their feelings comes from the belief that it will rebound on family. They might think that by admitting their struggle they're letting their loved ones down; that they're not providing what they should – i.e. strength and security. If you've always thought of yourself as a provider, and then the carpet's pulled from under your feet, be it losing your job, something going wrong with your health, feeling anxious about everything, or whatever, then you're going to suffer difficulties – and you need to tell someone. Instead you hear about people going to the park or sitting in their car every day because they can't admit they haven't got a job. Or getting hopelessly behind at work because they haven't got the mental energy to cope. People might see that silence as self-protection. Actually, in that person's head, they're protecting everyone else around them. Men often believe that by unburdening themselves they're just throwing that weight on to someone else. It's mad when you think about it. Because of a few crazy core beliefs, we just let ourselves slide deeper and deeper into desperation. It's a horrible place to be.

While I'll always be glad I opened up, I don't push people to do so, because I don't think that works. They need to feel the time has come to do so themselves. I get also that a lot of men will balk at the idea of sitting in a doctor's office, talking about their mental health. That's not for me either. There's a formality to it that puts me off. I'd much rather go for a chat in a café or a bite to eat. Something more normal and low-key. I don't think I'd tell the truth in that one-to-one serious environment because it's majorly out of my comfort zone. Doctors' surgeries are where you have blood tests or a finger up your arse. The good news is that mental health professionals are aware of this and so create as comfortable an environment as possible.

I'm aware also that at the wrong time people can take advice as criticism. If you've had a bad day, for example, you see advice as someone having a go. Twenty-four hours later, when you've cooled off and are seeing things more realistically, you do start to look at it in the way it was meant. I'd learned that lesson through football. A manager who comes in at half-time and blasts everyone in a five-mile radius immediately loses the confidence of players – the strikers, the wingers, the goalkeeper. Terry Venables never did that. If you'd done something wrong, he'd tell you, but then if you'd done something right, he'd make that into the bigger point. I'll give you an example. At half-time one year, Spurs were winning 1–0 away at Arsenal, the biggest game of the season. My once gleaming white shirt was covered in mud, and when you're covered in dirt, you always think you've played brilliant. 'Look at me!' you think. 'It's everywhere! I must have been fantastic!'

Terry wasn't quite so impressed. 'You know Bobby Moore?' he asked me.

'Yes,' I replied (this was even better than I thought – Terry was about to compare me to the greatest defender England ever had).

'He never got dirty once. You know why?'

'No,' I said, suddenly very interested in the pattern on the floor.

'Because he never got out of position.'

I was about to drown myself in the team bath when he added: 'I tell you what though, son – blinding tackle!'

The best managers know the difference between advice and criticism at the right time.

If you think you've got a mate who's struggling, the best thing to do is go slowly. Sit down with them and tell them you're there for them if they need anything. Don't be frustrated if they won't open up straightaway. Everybody's different. Give people space and assure them you're in their corner. Just doing that makes such a difference. Remember, they might have felt totally alone until that point. Now you've pushed the door open they can see there are people out there who want to help, who aren't judging them, and will do all they can to bring them out the other side.

If you're that person who needs help, but don't know how to go about it, I'd always advise that you talk to an older person who you trust. They're the ones who've lived life, who've got experience. They'll understand exactly what you're saying because they've seen so many ups and downs themselves. It doesn't matter that they haven't been through exactly what you're going through, they'll have been through a version of it. They'll know what it is to feel lonely or down or helpless. It also doesn't matter how successful they've been in life. I know players who've scored forty goals in a season – it doesn't mean they haven't had problems along the way. As a footballer, you spend three hours a week tops on the pitch. What about the other 165? Yes, there are people who breeze through life, but equally, there are a lot who don't. We shouldn't make assumptions about who might be able to help us.

Sadly, while the message is getting out there now that being honest about your feelings is nothing to be ashamed of, I do still expect there are some places in football where it's seen as a sign of weakness. All it takes is a toxic signal from a manager, some lazy words about toughening up or not 'behaving like girls', and the damage is done. There'll be hundreds of teams where that attitude prevails, thousands of blokes left feeling they don't have a voice, bottling stuff up, not wanting to be the one who speaks up in case they get humiliated in front of everyone else. That has to stop. It is so, so damaging. From top to bottom in football, we need to make sure that people feel comfortable in their environment and, if and when the time comes, can rely on others to help. That extends to the kids as well, because while a handful of them will go on to live their dream as a professional, many thousands more won't. What about them? What about those youngsters who are devastated and carry the weight of failure? Again, most likely it's hidden away inside. Clubs recruit 8-year-olds who dream of making it big, and then at 16, they find themselves on the scrapheap. That's thousands of kids. What's going through their heads? How can you expect a kid to handle that? You hear about some terrible tragedies happening after kids have gone through the trauma of a shattered dream.

From that point of view, I was one of the lucky ones. It was clear pretty early on that I'd be joining Millwall and that was the end of it. I had no worries on the 'getting picked up' front. My worries came later on. Looking back, maybe I didn't hide them as well as I always thought. I reckon a few people knew that somewhere below all the bluster I was having issues. After all, how different could we all be? Who actually leads a problem-free life? Think about it, if you put thirty people of any description in a room together they're going to have all sorts of difficulties and a football changing-room is no different. Chances are pretty much everyone I ever got changed alongside had their own things to deal with. And, like me, they weren't going to start shouting them from the rooftops in front of everyone.

There was one part of my make-up that others could definitely see. While I was the biggest, loudest person in the dressing room, I was quite a soft character underneath. I never really fell out with anyone, never had a bust-up with a teammate. That meant if anyone had a problem they came to me. I was the go-between, the link between the players and the manager, and was more than happy to do that, to offer that arm around the shoulder.

Sometimes my own shoulder would be required for a fellow player to cry on – at the manager's request. 'Razor,' a gaffer would say, 'go and have a word with him. Find out what's wrong.' They'd want me to be a father figure to the young lads coming through, or those, like Stan Collymore, who were deemed to be troublemakers. Other players at Liverpool thought Stan was a pain in the arse. They'd talk about him behind his back and didn't appreciate his unwillingness to join in with life off the pitch. But I could see there was a lot more to him. He wasn't trouble – he was troubled.

He needed someone to trust, someone who knew what it was like to be judged, to be thought of in a one-dimensional way. Who could that be, I wonder? When Stan got himself wound up, I'd sit with him, talking to him, squeezing his hands. 'You're going to get through this, mate. Everything's going to be all right.'

In the end, Stan started calling me 'Daddy hands'. If someone was having a go at him, I'd drag him away and sit with him. Where it came from, I don't know. Maybe my dad used to do the same with me, I don't remember. But I'd sit there, just squeezing and squeezing. Thinking about it, I'd come up with a similar squeezing technique to stop myself losing it on the pitch. Before a game, I'd attach some strapping to my hand and when I could feel the red mist rising, I'd pull it so it nipped my skin. The pain would snap me out of it. I've since heard that putting an elastic band on your wrist and snapping it against your skin to veer yourself away from negative thoughts is recommended by psychologists. Clearly, I was ahead of my time.

For a shit-stirrer on the pitch I was a very good peacemaker off it. If there was a fight among the lads, more often than not I was the one in the middle trying to break it up. There was one epic occasion involving Stan, a chair, and the goalkeeper Tony Warner, better known as 'Tony Bonus' because he never played a first team game for Liverpool but made 120 appearances on the bench, pocketing a tidy few quid every time we won. The clash came in the dressing room just before a game. The spark? Roy Evans making a comment about Stan not being aggressive enough. I'm not sure why Tony was the one on the end of Stan's ensuing rage but he came at him with the chair and I was somewhere in the middle, getting smashed to hell. 'All right, you pair, have you finished?'

It was the same if ever there was a training ground bust-up. When John Hartson and Eyal Berkovic had – how shall I put this? – a 'bit of a falling-out' during a West Ham practice session, again it was me who, in the manner of the very best boxing referee, stepped in to see if one party (Eyal) was OK and then ushered the other (John) away. Sadly the altercation, which had started when John's tackle from behind had prompted Eyal to throw his arm out in retaliation, only for John to then aim a kick which caught Eyal on the head, had been captured on camera for the world to see. Take a look – I'm right there, about five feet away. The angle made it look like John was using Eyal's bonce for volleying practice and the Welshman regretted it straightaway. The pair made up pretty quickly, but it was a stain on his reputation that John carried with him forever.

While I did once clock Robbie Fowler at an airport, I don't recall ever getting involved in a training ground bust-up at a football club. And to be fair, the Robbie thing was the result of a case of mistaken identity. Flights home from European games were generally a good excuse for a piss-up and the one back from Vladikavkaz in Russia after a UEFA Cup first round tie should have been no different. What made it different was that our defender Steve Harkness decided to take advantage of a slumbering Robbie Fowler by pissing in the shoes he'd shoved under his seat. As you can imagine, the feeling Robbie had when he woke up and put his shoes back on wasn't hugely to his liking. When he enquired as to who'd used his shoes as a urinal, the rest of the lads pointed at the now-sleeping me. Robbie, looking for a footwear-based revenge, gutted and filleted a £300 pair of Gucci boots he found in my stuff. When we landed there was a bit of an altercation on the runway. I thought he should buy me some new boots, he felt otherwise, and not being in the mood for a debate I landed one on him. The trail of blood went straight through to the luggage car-ousel. Within twenty-four hours it was all forgotten, although we do still make sure to keep our shoes on whenever we meet.

People always say footballers are stupid. I've had it said about me plenty of times – thanks, Colin – but I think it's fair to say, shoe-related airport incidents aside, I've shown a bit of intelligence for people around me, especially when it comes to how they might be feeling on the inside. I'd make discreet enquiries when I saw other players' wives. 'Er, your husband, how is he? Everything all right?' I know. Me, discreet. Who'd have thought it? A lot of players never talked to the other wives. If anything they were pretty dismissive of them. But somehow it was natural for me. I understood the value of a few words. Maybe subconsciously I'd taken in what Terry Venables used to do at Spurs. I'm not trying to big myself up – half the time I expect they just wanted me to go away – but it was just how I was. And people did open up to me. Forget *Wife Swap* and *Big Brother*, I really should have had one of those *On The Couch* type TV shows.

Then again, maybe not – my guidance wasn't always what you'd call orthodox. Take my advice to people who were fed up of being on the receiving end of piss-taking from another player. I used to say to them that if someone was having a go at them, they should stand up for themselves and have a go back. Football changing rooms are ruthless. If someone says, 'I fucked your mum', the answer isn't to walk away. It's to say,

'Yeah? Well, I fucked your mum's mum's mum's mum's mum – and then I fucked your dad's mum too.' That's so stupid the whole ridiculous argument collapses and everyone becomes mates again. It really is only a matter of time before I'm asked to lecture on a leading psychology course.

It's like finding out if someone's OK. I'd never say, 'Come on, mate, how about me and you have a proper good chat about what's going on in your life?' The better way of getting someone to open up is to be relaxed and give them an opportunity. If I go, 'Bloody hell, I've had a hell of a weekend', that's the perfect tee-up for them to say, 'Yeah, me too . . .' and tell me all about whatever's been bothering them. I'll have a bit of a to and fro with someone and let them reveal their problems without even realising it.

'Banter' has become a bit of a bad word in recent times but actually it has got its uses. You're not using it to put someone down, you're using it as a way of lifting them up. I never thought about it much as a footballer – I just did it and got on with it – but actually looking back, I do think it's quite clever. I was the first ever banter psychologist, or bantologist if you like. *The Bantologist* – forget JFK and cooking, there's my next book right there! It's not only football where that can work. It might happen down the pub, in an office, anywhere.

Mentioning something going wrong in your own life is a great way of subtly encouraging others around you to open up.

Thing is, while as a player I was always more than happy being the man in the middle, who does the go-between go to? Who puts the arm around them? I was left to deal with my troubles, my feelings of hopelessness, on my own. 'Snap out of it, Razor!' I'd tell myself. 'What's the matter with you?' But I knew only too well it doesn't work like that. And I was hardly going to go looking for help. Like I say, if professional football had taught me anything, it was that owning up to problems was an absolute no-no. Fracture an ankle and people could see you were broken. Mental scars were hidden. If you were going mad, you did it alone.

Occasionally during training I'd see a player totally lose it – shouting, swearing, kicking stuff around – and then just clear off. Gone – screeching out of the car park. Whether that was because of frustration or anger or something a bit deeper it's hard to say because, as I've pointed out, no-one ever fronted up as to how they were really feeling. But it was clear that the only way they could deal with what was boiling up in their head was to get away. I actually did it once myself, at Liverpool, in a training session with Sammy Lee, an ex-Red who I saw as a friend before a coach. I can't recall just what was making me feel so pissed off on that particular day but I really couldn't face doing the training. I turned towards the changing rooms: 'I'm fucking going in.'

'Don't you do it!' warned Sammy. 'Don't you go in!' But I did. I got changed and drove off while everyone else was still training. Madness, but I knew for my own sanity I had to do it. I knew I needed to find some kind of release.

Before I began opening up and had a better understanding of myself, some of the stuff that went round in my head was pretty dark. I used to chew over the music I'd have at my funeral. 'I'll show them,' I'd think. 'I'll pick a song that'll tell everyone what I was really thinking.' That's not right, is it? But at the same time I never considered myself depressed. 'Me? Depressed? I'm Razor Ruddock. I don't get depressed. People with no bottle get depressed.' As you can see, I really didn't like the word 'depression'. And if I'm honest, I still don't. The thought of depression makes me depressed. Depression to me is feeling sorry for yourself. I know that's wrong, and I don't mean to belittle other people's experiences, but I want to be honest about what 'depression' means in my head. When describing how I've felt over the years, I prefer to say 'down in the dumps'. But whatever you want to call it, it happened on a regular basis. Thinking about my kids from my first marriage and how long it had been since I'd seen them was a definite trigger. Other times I'd get teary when watching stuff on TV, again especially if it reminded me of the kids. When no-one was around I'd often find myself sat there with my head in my hands, thinking about them. Other times I'd just go to bed – if I was asleep, I couldn't be thinking about everything that was wrong. Some days I'd only be up a couple of hours. It seemed like the perfect escape, except of course what would happen then was I'd dream about them instead. I'd wake up feeling worse than when I'd crawled between the sheets.

The divorce from my first wife went on for years and years, with all the court battles you'd expect, and so was bound to affect my mood. Going out or playing golf could take those hard-to-handle feelings away. If my mind was busy, I was OK. But once I was sat at home again it was a whole different ballgame. Problem was, the more I sat there thinking and thinking, the same stuff going round and round in my head, the harder it would be to make myself go out. At that point, days, even weeks, would pass where I wouldn't want to speak to anyone. And of course, me being me, I kept all that stuff hidden inside. Leah would ask, 'Are you all right?' And I'd be like, 'Yeah, of course I'm all right.' It's much easier to do that than to start talking about what's going on in your head, same as I wasn't telling my mates how I really felt either. Telling them how you really are doesn't feel like an option. Who wants to hear that? Of course, things would actually be a lot better if we did speak up. If we gave those mates a chance to be what they are – mates. It doesn't mean the end of the fun and games. Me and my friends know we can have a serious conversation on a night out and still have a great time. That serious bit might be five minutes, it might be an hour, but I can guarantee the rest of the night will be as full of piss-taking and laughter as it ever was. Let's face it, what blokes are very good at is black humour. When I went in for the gastric sleeve operation, I had several requests for my set of Ping golf clubs, should I die.

Death had actually very much been on their minds. When I was at my biggest, if I was away speaking at a dinner one pal would make me ring on the way home to make sure I was OK. Or if I was staying over, he'd be like, 'What time did you get to bed?', meaning, 'You didn't get too pissed, did you?' We laugh about it now, but that's how frightened he was. I'd have been the same had it been the other way round. When you're that weight you're only one big night away from a proper bad fall; one hot, boozy, speaking engagement away from a coronary. I had a good few heart-to-hearts with this particular mate which helped me see the cycle I was in and how I'd pulled down the shutters against people giving me sound advice. Such as lose a shitload of weight. It's lovely to see how pleased other people are with the progress I've made, and at the same time it's hard because I've come to realise how worried they were. I hope people will read this, listen and break their own cycle before they face death's door.

By looking out for me, that friend became my parachute. The bloke I'm talking about is the same one who I tried to talk me out of giving up drink. As you can see, I came to understand just how mad that was. I realised the value of honesty. These days we're each other's parachute. By helping each other we know we're going to have a safe landing. No more crashing to the ground. I hope there are people out there who will realise their own parachute is nearer to hand than they might ever have imagined. Chances are it's been sitting right next to them for years – a friend, a relative, a colleague.

You can also use this book as a parachute. Not literally – you'll die. But if reading about how I stopped my own plummet to earth helps in some way, then I'll be the happiest ex-overweight, ex-footballer around.

12

A SAVIOUR IN IRAQ

While being a footballer is clearly a bit of a cul-de-sac career, with the occasional pathway into management, punditry, after-dinner speaking, reality TV, or in George Weah's case, president of Liberia, it's struck me while writing this book just how many strange, bizarre and uniquely challenging experiences footballers have in their locker that could prove a gateway into a different kind of existence.

How many people in normal life, for example, have slipped and done the splits at Ayresome Park on a wet Tuesday night and torn open their arsehole? Not many, I'll bet. It hurts by the way, tearing your arsehole, especially since in my case a lot of the blood went straight into my bollocks and I had to have it syringed out. I'm not sure what was worse, that or having my bum sewn up. It was like the aftermath of having a baby. I've still got stretch marks inside my legs.

Maybe that's not the best example of a professional foot-balling experience with job potential going forward – I'm useless with a needle – but I've definitely seen a side of life shared by few others. Playing in Europe, for instance, I'd some-times end up in distant places like Georgia or Azerbaijan. Such trips can be an eye-opener. When I went to Zagreb in Croatia with West Ham, our central defender Igor Stimac introduced the team to a load of his soldier mates, who promptly put us in the back of a wagon and took us out shooting handguns and AK-47s in the forest. It was mayhem. Bullets flying every-where, bits of trees splintering off. That, incidentally, was the morning of the match. It worked for me – I scored that night! 'What did you do before the game?' 'Oh, just blasted a load of bullets round a wood. No dramas.' People were chucking cans in the air while someone else tried to shoot them.

Imagine if that happened now. People would think we were mad. There'd be an international incident. Footballers, though, are used to crazy places and crazy people. We can go anywhere and be totally unfazed. Look at my old boss, Graeme Souness. When his Galatasaray side beat arch-rivals Fenerbahce in the Turkish Cup, he grabbed a Galatasaray flag, marched straight out in front of thousands of baying fans and planted it in the middle of the pitch. A lifetime as a footballer had taught him how to act in that situation. Had he not played in the Old Firm derby, he'd not have had a clue.

In my case, it was my skill as Razor, honed in football dressing rooms across the land, which took me into an actual warzone, heading off on a trip to Iraq with Combined Services Entertainment (CSE) to meet the British soldiers out there, at the same time reminding myself there are people fighting proper battles in this world. Forget footballers, these are the real heroes.

I'd been out to Iraq with CSE, which had long been providing light relief for British soldiers, a few times, but this 2005 trip would be different, because it was there I would meet a saviour, in the unlikely form of a *Playboy* Centrefold of the Year. Actually, I'm a footballer, so it's not unlikely at all. Getting together with models is a longstanding British footballing tradition. I fully expect the First Division's top scorer in 1889 was stepping out with the winner of Ankle of the Year. It's kind of what we do.

People have often asked about Leah's first impression of me and she always answers the same way: 'Look at the size of his fucking head!' Despite that, I was able to wear her down with my good looks, impeccable fashion sense and winning banter. OK, it also didn't hurt that she likes the older man.

She's fourteen years younger than me. In fact, I'm six months older than her stepdad. But I've never thought of myself as being the age that I am. I still think in my head that I'm somewhere in my mid-twenties. Some might be surprised to hear it's that old.

I'm not sure what attracted me to this beautiful, blonde, successful model with the world at her feet, but whatever her allure, it was definitely the first time I'd met anyone with their head screwed on so tight. In her game she'd had to be tough and she'd had to be clever. I compare modelling to being a footballer – there's always someone lurking, waiting to take advantage. No-one ever got near to doing that with Leah, she'd suss someone out before they'd even walked in the room. As a model, meanwhile, she'd been thrown every line in the book. She'd go out and find herself surrounded by blokes. When we got together properly back in the UK, a mate would say to me, 'Aren't you worried?' And I'd say, 'No, mate. Not in the least. She's heard it all before. It's me she's coming home with.'

Sometimes she'd shout over to me, 'Razor! This bloke says I should tell you to jog on. What does that mean?' My mates would be telling me to get over there and sort him out, but I knew she was just playing daft for a laugh. That's why she's been my best mate from the moment I met her – we've always been able to have a laugh together. Even now she winds me up. We were out for an Italian the other night. 'Ooh! Look at him!' she said, eyeing up the waiter. 'Oi!' I said, 'I am here, you know!' The poor bloke couldn't apologise enough. It wasn't his fault he had a giant pepperpot.

Leah's my wife, but she's also my backbone. It was the worst moment of my life when I almost lost her after she went into hospital to have our second daughter Kizzy. The nightmare began when she was struck by a really intense pain. Initially it was dismissed as just being part of the contractions, but it was so much worse than that. Leah was clearly in a bad way and a few quick investigations revealed she had internal bleeding. They opened her up and sorted it out. Great – except unknown to everyone she actually had two internal bleeds. They'd only found one. We'd not been home long when she was rushed back to hospital and straight into intensive care. She lost three-quarters of her blood. A doctor actually said to me, 'I don't think she's going to make it. You need to say goodbye.'

Leah's mum told me later that the colour completely drained out of me. I walked into intensive care and saw the woman I loved hooked up to all these bleeping machines. I was literally on the floor crying. I wasn't just saying goodbye to my beautiful soulmate, I was saying goodbye to the mother of a little girl who at that point I hadn't even seen. I felt so helpless. I wanted to save her – that was my job – but I didn't know what to do. The only thing that could save her was specialist surgery. Problem was the only surgeon equipped to do the operation was heading abroad that day. Leah's only here now because of the biggest dose of good luck anyone could ever have. The surgeon had actually forgotten something he needed on the trip and came back into the hospital to fetch it. Before he worked his miracle, I really did think I was going to say goodbye to Leah forever. I thought she was gone. I had a vision of walking away from that hospital with a newborn baby and no partner. Even now I don't know how she's here, I really don't. We both have a million questions about what went wrong that day, but whatever it was, we can be thankful that her coming through the other side was meant to be.

Why Kizzy? It's a name I always remembered from the TV mini-series *Roots* when I was a kid. Pebbles, meanwhile, comes from *The Flintstones*, although she did once ask, 'Did you call me Pebbles because I was conceived on Hastings beach?' (Leah's from Hastings.) I'll scotch that rumour once and for all right now. It was Bognor Regis. Only joking. I think.

Everything we'd been through as a family made mine and Leah's wedding day even more special. From that first meeting in Iraq, we'd waited nearly a decade to get married because we so wanted Pebbles and Kizzy to be part of the big day. As we danced to Barry White's 'Just the Way You Are' I felt overwhelmed by happiness. I wasn't to know the battle looming on the horizon ahead, and I wasn't to know the huge part the woman in my arms would play in dragging me through to the other side.

When it comes to Leah's front-row view of that battle, it would be wrong for me to try to describe her feelings for her, but reading her memories (below) has brought me to tears.

LEAH'S STORY

I used to lie next to Razor. Not sleeping, just staring into the darkness. 'What if he doesn't wake up in the morning?' I'd look over at him. 'I used to watch you on TV. I used to stick your picture in my Panini album, looking all handsome and lovely.' I'd allow myself a little smile at the memory. Ian Rush was the sticker I always wanted. He was the one I had a crush on. I've always had strange taste in men – look who I ended up with!

I should have known from the start that being with Razor was going to be – how shall I put this? – unusual. When I first clapped eyes on him in Iraq (just so you know, I've heard every joke going about me, Razor and warzones), he was enjoying a can of Heineken. Dressed from head to toe in pink, I was pretty hard to miss and when I grabbed one for myself he took the chance to butter me up with a bit of sweet-talk: 'Oi, you've nicked my Heineken!' I didn't reply – I was too taken aback by the size of his head.

I'd travelled out there with my best friend and fellow model, Jo Guest. I wasn't meant to be there at all but another girl got last-minute nerves and so I agreed to step in. The idea was to give soldiers serving abroad a bit of a morale boost – have a picture with a well-known face, something to stick in their pocket and maybe cheer them up a bit when they were home-sick. Fair to say Razor wanted more than a photo. He told me he was going through a divorce and made no secret that he fancied me. In fact, he was all over me like beans on toast. When we were taken on a tour of Saddam Hussein's palace he made his move. Only Razor would look at Saddam Hussein's bed and think of seduction. Another time we were having a kiss and a cuddle around the corner from the barracks when a load of soldiers walked past. You can imagine the reaction we got.

When we got back from Iraq, Razor asked for my number but I was a bit nervous about getting more involved. I'd always said to my friends that I'd never ever get together with a footballer – let's face it, the footballer and the model is the ultimate cliché – and so I gave him a fake number. He wasn't daft, he rang it straightaway, right in front of me. Maybe he had a history of women giving him the wrong number! If he hadn't done that, chances are I'd never have seen him again. Instead, I agreed to meet him the next day. Even then it was only to impress my brothers. Both are massive Liverpool fans and neither would believe me when I said who I'd met in Iraq. They thought I'd made the whole thing up. When Razor turned up in this massive black BMW they were gobsmacked. So it's thanks to them really that we got together properly at all.

I got to see quickly why Razor was so loved. He was a big friendly bear. The softest bloke you'll ever meet. He always had time for people. At the start, we'd go out for dinner and fans would constantly be asking for a photo. Not once did he ever say no. He had time for everyone and that told me a lot about him as a person. I'll admit that after a while I was getting a bit fed up of it. But then I thought about it and actually it was really nice that people had so much affection for a bloke that even though he'd finished playing, they still wanted an excuse to say hello. I'd done a lot of high-profile modelling work, F1 and all that kind of stuff, but being with Razor was a whole different world to get used to. Everyone wanted a slice of him. Everywhere we went I'd hear a shout of 'Razor!' It's why I call him Razor myself. That's what everyone called him when we met.

I soon realised as well that footballers and models aren't that bad a fit. We have more in common than you might think. For one thing, me and Razor both lived lives where we were judged. We knew how that felt, the pressure it could bring. For another, the career trajectory is the same. For a while you're in the limelight, the bee's knees, and then all of a sudden that's it, you're considered over the hill.

I actually gave up a lot of work after I met Razor. My agent rang me one day: 'We've got a cricket team on an open-topped bus. Can you make it?' I said no.

Razor was amazed. 'You do know that was the England cricket team – the Ashes-winning England cricket team? Why did you turn it down?'

'Because I'm in bed with you.'

Laughter's always been the strongest part of our relationship. I do sometimes think, 'How the bloody hell did we get this far?' But I know it's because he's always had that ability to make me laugh. I mean real, proper, belly laughs. And I do the same to him. We need that side of each other so much. Which made it so hard when it stopped.

It felt like the heavier Razor got, the more he withdrew into himself. He would sleep a lot in the day, blaming it on an old footballing habit when I asked, but I knew there was something more to it, that he wasn't right in himself. He was hard to live with for so long. He didn't really say a lot to anybody. He never used to smile. And he stopped taking care of himself, not shaving, not bothering about what he was wearing. I used to look at him and think, 'How have you let yourself get like that?' Which I know is awful – and of course I loved him regardless – but it was hard for me to see, and even harder for the kids. They'd ask me again and again, 'Is he going to be all right?' I'd tell him how worried they were but he'd just brush it off: 'I'm fine. I'm fine.' He was Razor Ruddock – and Razor Ruddock is indestructible. At least that's what he was telling himself. Whether he actually believed it is something else altogether. After all, by then he'd started humming when he went upstairs to cover up his puffing and panting. I'd been with him for the best part of twenty years. Was I supposed to believe he'd sud-denly taken up humming when going upstairs? His mobility was so bad he wasn't far off having a bed downstairs. I'm so glad he didn't because I think that could, in his mind, have been the moment of no return. When he abandoned himself to his fate.

The amount he was eating, and the lack of care about what he ate, was shocking. If he went to the Chinese, he'd come back with loads of different dishes. The table would be absolutely heaving. Other times he'd make a piece of toast and absolutely smother it with butter. I'd be watching him. 'What do you think you're doing?' I'd get the knife, scrape it off and put it back in the tub. I know that sounds controlling, but it's not. I was doing it for his health. I was desperate as his wife to do something good. I'd say, 'Let's go for a nice walk today.' But he'd just shrug. Another day would pass without anything positive happening. I was in a really difficult position. Because I was telling him again and again that he had to look after himself, I felt like I'd become this horrible nagging wife. It would make me feel bad, but I just couldn't understand how he'd become so blind to what was around him – a loving wife, a good life, two beautiful children – in his case, four beautiful children. So why did he feel so bad? It's hard not to put that on yourself. Sometimes I'd wonder if he even wanted to be with me anymore; random times when I even wondered if it would be better if I left. But then I'd think, 'How can I leave what we started all those years ago? And what will happen to him if I do?' I stayed because I love him – because what I was actually doing was trying to save his life. And I did save his life. I really don't think he'd be here now if I'd not stuck with him in those darker times. He needed someone to be with him, to be by his side and on his side.

It's obvious to me that Razor was depressed. He'll say 'down in the dumps', but he was depressed. Of course he was, although I don't think even now he'd admit it. It seems too big a barrier for him to use that word. He was depressed because he was heavy, and he was heavy because he was depressed. The two things fed each other. It was a totally toxic cycle he was trapped in. I'd worry about him all the time. He was desperately ill, like his body had given up. The whites of his eyes had turned yellow. The skin around them was pasty and puffy. He had so much fat round his neck that he used to speak like he was talking into a bucket. I'd look at him, barely able to believe the fit and healthy sportsperson he once was. I'd remind him that he wasn't 25 anymore; that he wasn't inde-structible. Again he'd repeat those words, 'I'm fine. I'm fine,' but *from where I was sitting he was borderline dead. Lockdown only made matters worse. We've all done it – reached for the comfort food when we feel down or stressed – but this was something else. I did my best, cooking him the healthiest meals – open our fridge and it's like the salad counter at Waitrose – but the doorbell kept ringing, the takeaways kept arriving. There were times when it felt like a slow death.*

It's awful to watch someone you love slip away. Even more so when all you hear is other people's nasty comments. If I walked a few steps behind Razor I'd catch them all. 'Fucking size of him!' 'Jesus, what the fuck's happened to Razor Ruddock?' And I just had to listen to it. If I wasn't hearing it in the street, I was seeing it on social media. In the beginning, I couldn't take it. I wanted to punch somebody. Razor says it never bothered him. I'm not so sure. If ninety-nine people say something good about you and one says something horrible, it's always the bad one you find yourself thinking about in the middle of the night. Right now, there'll be people out there waiting for him to put weight back on. Why people feel the need to be so negative, so destructive, I don't know.

As if that wasn't bad enough, I'd get strangers constantly telling me, 'Look at him! You've got to do something!', as if I wasn't trying. Thing is, you can't make somebody do something if they don't want to do it themselves. It's why in some ways the whole Harry's Heroes *thing – the way it's portrayed as being the catalyst for Razor's big mental shift – isn't quite what it seems. When Paul Merson said his piece to Razor, it looked like that was the first time anyone had ever challenged him about what he was doing to himself, but the reality was I'd been doing it, chipping away at those same challenges, for years.* Harry's Heroes *was the catalyst for Razor getting the medical advice which led to him getting a pacemaker but the underlying issues of his weight and mood remained.*

For me, the most powerful part of the whole Harry's Heroes *experience was when David Ginola came over to me off camera. David understood how fragile life can be, having suffered a heart attack during a charity match and being clinically dead for eight minutes. And that was as a supposedly fit and healthy man. He wasn't carrying the weight that Razor was.*

'I'm genuinely worried,' he told me. 'You don't have to be 27 stones, it can happen to anybody.'

He was only telling me what I already knew. In all honesty, I don't understand how Razor escaped a heart attack. For so long he must have been right on the edge. If he hadn't faced up to what was happening, he wouldn't be here now.

While Razor talks about the picture of himself underneath the dartboard as a big moment of realisation, it was a photo of him during a 'Quit Smoking' campaign that really shocked me, really brought home to me just how big he'd got, so much so that I actually thought it had been photoshopped – that somebody had blown it up. But no, that really was him. I actually sent that photo to the gastric sleeve surgeon to emphasise just how desperately we needed his help.

Even then, when the gastric sleeve plan was revealed, we got stick on social media: 'Why can't he go to the gym to lose weight like everyone else?' He had actually done that before he'd had the pacemaker fitted – doing the battle ropes and everything – and without knowing it nearly killed himself. He didn't have the option to put himself under that kind of strain again. Because he had a pacemaker there was no other way apart from surgery. And anyway since when has losing weight been a competition? What is this – do it the gym way or it doesn't count? Those people hiding behind their keyboards weren't seeing what I was seeing; living what I was living. They weren't looking at the person they loved lying there in bed wearing a mask, checking how many times they stopped breathing during the night. The doctors told me he was dying in his sleep. Imagine lying next to someone you love who's dying several times a night. Razor had to wear that mask for months before they'd give him a gastric sleeve. It was the only way to make sure he wouldn't die on the operating table. And people were banging on about him 'cheating'?

I'm so proud of where Razor's at now. 'You've come a long way,' I tell him. And so have I. But I know as well there are millions more women like me out there still daily trying to deal with men like Razor. It makes me emotional thinking about the silent struggle those women are going through, living with men who don't listen, trying to be there for them, doing the best they can. So many women watching partners deteriorate physically and mentally because they're men and don't know how to deal with it – or even how to admit that it's happening in the first place.

What's often forgotten is us women are crying out for help too. When we've got a husband who's suffering, but won't admit it, we suffer as well. And the probability is we'll be keeping it quiet because we feel like we have to be strong for our bloke, that we're letting him down in some way if we talk about him to someone else. I know I kept so much inside and I'm sure other women will be doing exactly the same. Sometimes I wish I had a special phone which they could call me on and ask what they should do. I might not be the best person to talk to – I'm no expert in these things – but I do know exactly what they'll be feeling. They'll be totally lost, trying to deal with men who won't speak up, won't ask for help, won't be honest with themselves or the people who love them. Razor was exactly that. He never ever asked for help. Not once. I'm actually writing this with tears in my eyes because I know how devastating silence can be. I had a childhood friend who took his own life. He kept his fears and worries bottled up on the inside. And then one day it was too late. That's the most powerful thing to come out of what's happened to Razor. The fact that someone like him can now look other men in the eye and say, 'Speaking up and asking for help is the best thing you can ever do.' He's a stronger person for being honest, same as I'm a stronger person for going through my own ordeal. I come from a long line of strong women, which gave me a head start when it came to this particular test, but it's not something any woman should ever have to go through.

I look at the new Razor. He's still a bear. Just not as big a bear. He's also got his looks back. I feel like I recognise him again. That sparkle in the eye is there – worryingly! – and he tells me he loves me every day. More than anything, he's so much fun. Down the years our girls have seen him sad, they've seen him struggle. There were times when he was heavy when he couldn't do all the normal things with them, like have a wander round the zoo, or mess around in the garden, and I do think he's carried a bit of guilt around about that. But he's always tried to be the best dad he can be. He's generous to a fault, but more than anything they've been spoiled with love.

I wish Razor would have counselling to keep his mental state level, but at the same time I can see how much he's worked out for himself. He knows he's had a close call, a few weeks away from death – it doesn't get much closer than that – and he knows his attitude to life has to change. Maybe in some ways I've been his counsellor. Bungo the counsellor. Bungo's his nickname for me, after the womble of the same name. Bungo was known for being a bit bossy, so that's probably what he was thinking at the time. But Bungo was also the one with all the ideas and a great sense of humour, so the joke's on him. Talking of which, the thing he's most happy about with the weight loss is that he can see his dick again. He's over the moon about it. Someone has to be.

Whatever it is that makes us rattle along so well together, it works. Whatever's been thrown at us, we've got through it. I'm proud of how hard we've both worked to get him to where he is now. When he was lost and overweight I'd have given anything for him to be like he is today. For it to actually happen is just amazing. If it hadn't, he wouldn't be here. I know what that feels like because there was a time when Razor was definitely gone. I don't know where he was, but he wasn't on this planet. Now Razor, the old Razor, the man I married, is back.

EPILOGUE

I've got a tattoo on my arm – *Seen it, done it, worn the shirt. Have you?!*

It's been a bit of a journey but finally I'm at peace with myself. I know how to live with Razor. I've learned how to be in the same room as him without having to spend the entire time in his grip. I see the world through my own eyes. I don't feel the need to see it through his. I've been given another trip round the block. Because, like Leah says, quite honestly, the way I was as Razor, I was on the way out.

I know as well that there remain, in all walks of life, many blokes who are still living a life – big nights out, drinking too much, eating crap – that inside they feel they've left behind. Some characters run their course. There's a timescale on parts of your life, parts of your character, and you have to accept that. You can't keep being that person. At some point they go back on the shelf and you become someone else. Unless you walk away, it won't just be you caught up in the fallout.

I hope this book can be a gentle nudge in the ribs that you don't have to be that same person year after year – that the judgement so many men fear if they throw off that armour of blokeishness will never appear. I'm a living, breathing example of that. Take last week when I caught up with my brothers Gary and Colin and a few old school pals. The fact I've spoken about my inner feelings, that I don't drink like I used to, don't stay out half the night, hasn't changed a thing. We still have a laugh, still take the piss out of each other. The only difference is how pleased and relieved they are that I've finally addressed the issues in my life that were dragging me down physically and mentally, same as I recognise the things they've had to deal with. We all know we can talk about anything.

One mate told me he loves me and is just so glad to have me back; how he really did fear I was going to die. There was a time when I'd have laughed at that kind of thing, made some stupid remark, just to make the discomfort of someone speaking so honestly go away. These days I'll take the time to appreciate what they're saying – and then take the piss! And they'd do the same to me. What I'm saying is, telling someone you give a shit doesn't have to be weird. It can be as normal as you want it to be. The bigger point is that you're being honest. You're changing that blokey dynamic that says all men talk about is sport and boozing. Hiding behind an image can never be right. Look at it this way, if you were hurt in a car crash, you wouldn't hide in the wreckage because you didn't want anyone to see your broken leg. So why is being hurt mentally any different? Put your hand up. Someone will be there to pull you out. Just ask. If there's just one person who reads this book who does exactly that, then writing it will have been worthwhile.

I know also that I've still got a way to go. For one, I need to stop smoking – probably the best thing anyone can do for their health. And their wallet. I don't just mean the prices of the things. Going outside for a fag in London has cost me a fortune over the years because, being a softie at heart, I always end up giving a homeless person a fiver. Not that I've always smoked. I actually started when I went on *I'm a Celebrity . . .* I noticed early on that the smokers were all getting ten fags a day. I also noticed that while I was starving all the time they didn't seem to be bothered. Either they were eating Benson & Hedges for breakfast or something else was going on. 'They stop you getting hungry,' they explained. That was it, I was straight in the hut to speak to the producers: 'Er, excuse me – you do know I smoke?' The first one made me feel dizzy and sick. I gave the rest of that day's supply to John Lydon. He reacted like I'd handed him a million quid. And I did get used to smoking. If it had been the American version, I could have sued the show for starting me off. OK, I did go and ask for the fags – but, I'd tell the beak, I had no choice, they were starving me!

It might sound strange that it took me so long to have a fag, but actually not many footballers lit up in my day. At Spurs, for example, there was only Ossie Ardiles, generally lighting one up at half-time, while at Liverpool, David James preferred to have one on the coach. Every journey was the same – 'Get away from me, Jamesy, you fucking stink!' As time went on and more and more European footballers came into the English league, the percentage of smokers gradually increased. Let's face it, Italians are born with a fag in their hand, same goes for the French. Doesn't seem to do them any harm. They've both won more World Cups than us.

Leah's said if I quit smoking I can go back in bed with her. To be fair, it's not a bad incentive. They better not make it available on the NHS! The good news is, I know there are much better ways to relax than tobacco. I've got five of them – a Labrador, Cockapoo, Chihuahua and two – get this

– Cockermatians (that's cocker spaniel Dalmatian crosses). A ladder must have been involved when the parents got together. I quite like having crossbreeds. Makes me feel better about the whole Neil/Razor thing.

Fags remain a challenge, but when it comes to the other battles I've overcome, the biggest thing for me is that the kids have got their dad back and Leah's got her husband back. That bloke sat there day after day down in the dumps has gone. Now they've got the me who likes to be laughing and having fun. If I feel myself slipping backwards I always think about them. They're my teammates now. I also think about Dad. I often look back on what he'd say to me if he saw me looking down in the dumps. 'Come on, son,' he'd tell me. 'You'll be OK.' I wonder what he'd think of me now, writing about this stuff. I hope, and think – actually I know – he'd be proud of me.

Of course, the threat of a return to those bad days of misbehaviour and mental turmoil is always there, but in all honesty, I don't expect to be slipping backwards now. I'm proud of myself. And when you're proud of yourself it's easier to keep something good going. When I wasn't proud of myself, that's when 'mad, bad, sad, glad' syndrome kicked in and I turned into Razor. I don't ever want to go back to that. I'll keep making myself proud by being the best version of myself to me, my friends, my family, and everyone I meet. Mad, bad, sad, glad – I'm still capable of being all of those things, the difference is I now know how to deal with each of them. It's taken me a long time, but finally I know who I am – head strong, body strong. I'll even walk to the furthest gate at Gatwick. Happily get out of the golf buggy. I'm up and down those fairways, no problem. I'm fitter. I'm healthier. I don't feel tired all the time. I've been given a second chance. Because, honestly, the way I was, I had no more rolls of the dice.

It's a big moment when you start to live again. I mean properly live, appreciating what you've got around you. It's like the blinkers have been taken off. Without getting too hippyish about it, you do start to appreciate the little stuff – the fresh air, a bit of birdsong while you're out with the dogs. I'm always happy finding out more about myself and what makes me tick. For instance, when I had my DNA tested for a TV show, the results came back saying I'm Scottish, English, Scandinavian and Japanese. Had I known that thirty years ago, I could have had a long and successful international career playing for the land of the rising sun.

I know what some people will say: 'Razor's gone soft. I preferred the Razor who was pissed up at Heathrow at 9 a.m.'

I'm fine with that. It's an easy way of dealing with something that's a bit out of the comfort zone. It's the sort of thing I'd have said myself a few years ago. But if that person digs a bit deeper I think they'll recognise at least a little bit of themselves in my story. I hope they'll think about opening the door on their deeper feelings, even if it's just the tiniest bit, because there's better times to be had on the other side. When you feel good in yourself, you feel good about yourself.

I mean, when you think about it, the things you look back on that make you proud in life aren't the endless sessions in this pub, the countless piss-ups in that one. In my personal life it's the fact I have four beautiful children. It's the fact I have a wife and friends who I love and who love me back. In my professional life, it's that I always tried my hardest on the pitch and always had time for people off it.

In fact, my brothers still like to remind me how they'd be stood in the freezing cold for an hour waiting while I signed autographs for kids outside Anfield. They'd see me give my washbag to one kid, my boots to another – 'Don't sell them, hang them on your bedroom wall!' Say what you like about me as a footballer, but I always tried to do that side of my job properly, because I can remember myself how big a deal it is to be looked in the eye and spoken to by someone you look up to. And I know how much it hurts when they ignore you and walk away. I never refuse a selfie precisely because of that.

The toxicity in my life came from things I added on to who I was. The challenge for me was to identify those elements and try to get rid of them. To undergo a detox. When we hear about people undergoing a process like that, usually we think of some reality show where people are chanting in a circle or having a tube full of coffee shoved up their arse. While I'm always a bit nervous when Leah gets the hosepipe out, for me the detox has been in the head. I've definitely got a suggestive personality. For instance, I'm really badly influenced by what I see on the telly. Someone in *EastEnders* having a fag? I want a fag. Ad for Guinness? That looks nice! McDonald's? Where's the Deliveroo app? The worst is putting a cooking programme on, watching some amazing dish being made. By the time the end credits roll, I've got my coat on and am heading off out to buy everything I need to cook it. I do that all the time. I'm so open to suggestion, I'm an advertiser's dream. The more serious side of being so open to suggestion is that growing up in football dressing rooms, environments where the loudest voice, the biggest drinker, the person with all the jokes and the stories is the one everybody loves wasn't the most helpful for me. Hardly a surprise that Razor became my character of choice. Now I have an understanding that it's OK to be a more realistic version of me. That friends and family love you for who you are – whatever. That people who care will never say, 'Get a pair of bollocks.' It's lovely to see how many people are proud of me.

Razor's the drug I've detoxed from. I don't need him anymore. My brothers got it right when they told me I act differently when I'm out these days, that I'll talk about different things. I can be Razor-ish when I want to be, but it's always on my terms. I control him, he doesn't control me. With Razor packaged away, I'm free to detox other areas of my life. I can build and rebuild relationships. I see food as something to be healthily enjoyed, not something that dulls bad feelings. I see a night out as a time to be with people I love, not a platform for a performance. I see my wife and children without the guilt that comes from knowing I could be so much more. I see life as smooth and happy, not an endless obstacle course.

For the first time in a long time I feel confident again. I believe that people want to know me, not Razor. Look at the way I talk about football. Beforehand I never thought that anyone would want to hear about what I know about the game, which is why I've always talked a lot more about the other stuff, the crazy things, the Razor things, that went on. Now I'm beginning to look at it a different way. I played for some of the biggest clubs in the country. I was good at what I did. And I've got a load of knowledge about it. I've come to see that I lived mine and every other kid's boyhood dream and people want to know how that feels. I'm glad I can finally do that without thinking I need to throw in a mad story three times a minute. I'm relaxed. I'm confident. I'm in a good place. I'M NORMAL! Neil 'Razor' Ruddock is normal! Don't believe me? Well, get this – I'm actually a founder member of the Norms, a little gang of blokes who all refer to one another as Norm – short for Normal. There's about sixteen of us now. When anyone new comes along, he too becomes a Norm. People think it must cause confusion, but actually it's the exact opposite. We've all found that whenever we say 'Oi! Norm?', the correct Norm always turns round. Try it yourself – form a group of Norms. It's 100 per cent the way forward.

I'm lucky to have so many great people around me who care. Gary and Colin are right up there on that list, and I hope they'll forgive me for not always showing my love for them in the most obvious ways. I'm reminded, for instance, of the time when I came out of the jungle on *I'm a Celebrity . . .* and was asked by a reporter if my campmate Jordan's were the two biggest tits I'd ever seen. 'Obviously you've never met my brothers,' I replied. Don't feel sorry for them. For years they called me Twiggy.

Then there were the times at Liverpool when they'd come and see me play and I'd leave them a couple of seats on the Kop at the ticket office. Only the very best seats for my brothers – nine quid a pop (at Millwall, I'd tell them to come at half-time because it was free). I used codewords at Liverpool, a lesson learned when I'd left tickets for Dad one week. Someone must have overheard him collecting them and the next time he came, they'd already gone. From then on I'd leave strict instructions with the ticket office that they should only give them out if the people collecting them got the right word. Dad would always collect his tickets under the name of Nick Faldo. When my brothers came one week I picked the name of a band. I informed the ticket office, but then 'forgot' to tell Gary and Colin. When they arrived, they were left spluttering their way through the pop and rock history of the world. 'Oasis?' 'No.' 'The Who?' 'No.' 'Fleetwood Mac?' 'No.' In the end they were sent to the back of the queue. I wasn't a complete twat – I told the ticket staff that if they hadn't got it by five past three, they should just let them in. I also said I'd never do it again. A few weeks later one of them was stood at the same hatch reeling off names of cartoon characters. 'Hong Kong Phooey?' 'Sorry, sir, you'll have to do better than that.'

Another time, Gary went to watch me at Manchester City v Liverpool with our brother-in-law, Craig. It was the usual fun and games at the ticket counter. By this time, Gary had had enough. When the bloke asked for the codeword he was ready to sack the whole thing off, get back on the train and go home.

'Hang on a minute,' said the ticket bloke, 'it says here Craig must answer.'

'Muff muncher,' said Craig. The bloke duly handed over the tickets.

I hope putting my brothers, two blokes who worked their bollocks off in life, through such a rigmarole to see their little brother who spent his days kicking a ball around didn't piss them off too much. I am grateful I've never worked a day in my life. Gary did ask me if I'd go to work with him one day, which I did, but crucially he never stipulated that I'd have to do something when I got there. So I didn't.

I will always be busy though, always looking for a bit of fun, a new experience in life. The London Marathon is out – luckily these days I have arthritis in both knees – but there is other uncharted territory. For instance, my intellectual powers have never been sought out by TV, a shame because I've always fancied taking the big chair in *Celebrity Master-mind*, especially now I can fit in it. Know what my specialist subject would be? *Titanic.* I can tell you the lot about the great liner – why they never saw the iceberg, how many dogs died, the breakfast menu in first class, everything. After my Cup Final experience at Liverpool, I also know how it feels to sink without trace.

I also haven't ruled out a pipe. I see myself in a cravat, undertaking a tour of provincial Victorian theatres, sat in a Chesterfield, with a crystal tumbler of whisky, puffing on my pipe – the original and best vape – recalling tales from my career and recreating my headbutt on Craig Short. If no-one comes, fine. Like I say, I'm happy in my own company. If Leah and the kids are out, I can spend hours sitting in my den with the dogs – big telly, photos on the walls. I could go on holiday on my own easy. Have a wander round, hour in a café, watch people. And I can always find a new friend if I want one. Anyone wants to talk about serious maritime disasters, I'm your man. There's an added bonus – these days I won't kidnap you and make you get drunk with me for a fortnight.

I'm also available for minor legal enquiries, having suc-
cessfully represented myself against the might of the British
legal system. I got caught by a camera speeding on the way
back from a sportsmen's dinner. The points I'd accrued would
have sent me over the twelve-point limit and mean an auto-
matic ban. Eventually, I was called to appear at magistrates'
court in Kidderminster. 'My lords,' I told them (I'd seen a
few episodes of *Judge John Deed*, I knew how these things
worked), 'I think you should know I never actually had the
letter informing me of the offence of which I'm accused. The
first I knew of this affair was when I received a letter telling
me I was guilty of not giving information.' Maybe it was the
kind of technicality that would see a shout of 'Case dismissed!'
and everyone concerned clear off home. Of course, courts
have become wise to these sorts of manoeuvres and so they
send for the relevant person from the police to come along
and produce the evidence, a note on a computer or whatever,
that the letter has been sent. Except in this case, they hadn't
turned up. Beautifully, the court itself had failed to send out
the letter requesting their attendance. With no witness, the
case collapsed. I was even awarded expenses for the fuel I'd
used driving to Kidderminster. I'd used quite a bit as well as
I'd had to drive fast to get there on time.

More tattoos? I think I possibly have enough. The one that stands out the most is on my arm, the motto of Liverpool Football Club – *You'll Never Walk Alone.* Hearing it sung as a player made the hairs on the back of my neck stand up. But I hear it now and I'm more like my mum, a few tears clouding the eyes, because finally I hear what it's really saying – that there will always be people who have your back, people who care, people whose strength you can draw on when you feel desperate and lost. There was a time in my life when I had so little love for myself, so much confusion about who I was, what I was meant to be, that I forgot those people were there. I withdrew into my shell so much that it took a lot of hard work from those same people to drag me out again into the clear fresh air. But eventually they did. They had never stopped trying. And that's the thing. Take a look out of that shell and you'll find everyone and everything you need to get you going again. They were there all the time.

Whoever we are, whatever our troubles, we never walk alone. I promise you it's true.

Acknowledgements

In any story of my life, there are two people I have to thank above and beyond anyone else: Mum and Dad. You both supported me tirelessly and I am so, so grateful for the massive part you have played in my life.

I would also like to say a special thank-you to my stepdad Larry, and brothers Colin and Gary (can we please now get over the fact I had steak while you had Spam?), and their wives, Alison and Sam.

To Lee Harlow Hanning – thanks, mate for all the chats. You've been an absolute saviour down the years, a wise head and a strong shoulder to lean on.

Tony Clarke and Paula from Soccer Speaker – thanks for everything.

Same goes for Ben Thomas at GIANT. So glad to have you and your family in my life.

I was lucky to grow up with a great group of mates and

ACKNOWLEDGEMENTS

I'm even luckier to still have them in my life. To you all, thank you.

Same goes for all the managers, coaches, players and fans who have supported me down the years.

I'd also like to mention Kingsnorth Golf Club – such a big part of my life.

Appreciation goes to Jonathan Taylor at Headline and James Wills at Watson Little for their belief in me and this book.

Finally, I'd like to say thank you to John Woodhouse for having the patience and courage to help me get through this project. Cheers, pal. I was only joking – the North's not so bad.

Photo Credits

Page

1 – all courtesy of the author.

2 – all courtesy of the author.

3 – top left: Professional Sport/Getty Images; top right: Getty Images; middle right: Mirrorpix/Getty Images; bottom left: Bob Thomas/Getty Images; bottom right: Colorsport/Shutterstock.

4 – top left: Colorsport/Shutterstock; top right: Graham Chadwick/Getty Images; bottom left: Liverpool FC/Getty Images; bottom right: Bob Thomas/Getty Images.

5 – top: Craig Prentis/Getty Images; middle: Laurence Griffiths/Getty Images; bottom: Phil Cole/Getty Images.

6 – top: Ken McKay/Shutterstock; middle: Cameron Laird/Shutterstock; bottom: Mike Marsland/Getty Images.

7 – all courtesy of the author.

8 – all courtesy of the author.